A YOUTHFUL LOVE
JANE AUSTEN AND TOM LEFROY?

A YOUTHFUL LOVE
JANE AUSTEN AND TOM LEFROY?

Nadia Radovici

MERLIN BOOKS

© Nadia Radovici 1995
First published in Great Britain 1995

British Library Cataloguing in Publication Data.
A catalogue record for this book is available from the British Library.

Published in Great Britain by
Merlin Books Ltd., Braunton, Devon

ISBN 0-86303-681-3

Printed in England by Orchard & Ind Ltd., Gloucester

To Lord and Lady Menuhin
this love story is dedicated

'Who knows ... where we are bound for, or why, or who sent us, or what we shall find — who knows anything, except that love is our faith — love...

Virginia Woolf inspired by Anne Thackeray-Ritchie

'Such excellent parents ... should be happy in their children's marriages ... so totally free from all those ambitious feelings which have led to so much misconduct and misery, both in young and old!'

Jane Austen, *Persuasion*

CONTENTS

Introduction	1
I. *Northanger Abbey* — The story behind the story	3
II. *Persuasion* — What Jane Austen wished to tell in her last novel	18
III. Somebody Jane Austen will never forget or forgive	36
IV. And what about the absent hero, Tom Lefroy?	48
Bibliography	80

INTRODUCTION

All Jane Austen's biographers, beginning with James Edward Austen-Leigh who wrote *A Memoir* about his aunt in 1869, up to Park Honan, author of the last important biography, *Jane Austen: Her Life*, written in 1987, have been unanimous in stating that Jane Austen's relationship with Tom Lefroy, nephew of Mrs Lefroy, a neighbour of the Austen family, had been a youthful love, a short flirtation and nothing more.

The romance was abruptly ended because Mrs Lefroy considered young Jane too poor for her nephew and she had the young man 'hurried away' in order to prevent more mischief.

The Austen family was always to consider the abrupt ending of the relationship between Jane and Tom Lefroy as a great wrong and efforts were made to hide Jane's grief and regrets from the world, turning the whole affair into a trifle.

The secrecy maintained on this subject for generations by the Austen family, as well as by the Lefroy family managed to convince posterity and this explains the general opinion adopted by all Jane Austen's biographers regarding her relationship with Tom Lefroy.

However, going attentively through the biographical details of the so-called 'eventless' life of Jane Austen, I gradually became convinced that her attachment for young Tom Lefroy had been strong and enduring, and that the grief that followed their parting was actually deep and lasting. *Northanger Abbey* and *Persuasion*, the first and the last of Jane Austen's novels, were to confirm my conviction.

And last but not least, in the *Memoir of Chief Justice Lefroy* by his son Thomas Lefroy, we learn what became of Tom Lefroy after he had given up the woman he dearly loved.

A last word to you, reader, in this little book you will discover a different Jane Austen from the one she generally is supposed to have been — and about whom another great English woman writer was mistaken to write:

> the passions are very unknown to her ... Even the feelings she vouchsafes no more than an occasional graceful but distant recognition ... Her business is not half so much with the human heart as with the human eyes, mouth, hands and feet ... What sees keenly, speaks aptly, moves flexibly it suits her to study; but what throbs fast and full though hidden ... this Miss Austen ignores ... She was a complete and sensible lady, but a very incomplete and rather insensible woman.

1 NORTHANGER ABBEY — THE STORY BEHIND THE STORY

'Only connect', P. L. Travers, the creator of Mary Poppins

Northanger Abbey has been characterized as the most explicitly literary of Jane Austen's novels: it is a novel about novels and novel-readers. Most of the novel's fun comes from the references to the Gothic novels and the influence which their reading had on the readers.

Nevertheless some critics have agreed 'that the Gothic burlesque is not well blended with the rest of the story. That Jane Austen added the Gothic passages to a plot originally concerned with a young lady's entrance into the world.' (Introduction to Northanger Abbey by Ann E. Ehrenpreis, Penguin, 1982, p.13)

This statement made me suspect that Jane Austen wanted to tell us a different story — *her* story, written in the period that followed a great disappointment. The date of that event and the writing of the novel more or less coincide.

And so I came to think that Northanger Abbey might be an autobiographical testimony, that the story behind Catherine Morland's tale of mystery and imagination, might — with some changes — be the account of what happened in real life between herself and her young Irish friend Tom Lefroy.

With these thoughts in mind I started to read Northanger Abbey again. And an amazing revelation took place: all that was fantasy and fiction slowly vanished in the background and only the very fabric of what might be the real life story — behind the novel — appeared as if in red letters. We may compare Northanger Abbey with a golden ring, embellished by a brightly coloured semi-precious stone: the stone is cut in diamond shape and catches the eye because it glitters, while the setting of pure gold passes unobserved.

In the novel the story that catches the reader's attention is the romantic episode in which the heroine Catherine Morland, because she has read too many Gothic novels, imagines the most dramatic events of murdered and captive ladies in Northanger Abbey.

With Jane Austen's life story in mind my attention was caught by the story behind the romantic episode. And this is the story we read: There was once a young girl, Jane or Catherine — never mind her name. She lived with her parents in a small village of cottages, 'a somewhat tame country, with quiet charm' (*A Memoir* by J. E. Austen-Leigh). Hers was a large, cheerful, and happy family. She had a happy nature. She was cheerful, modest, balanced and contented, grateful for everything life offered and had an open, genuine countenance.

But let Jane, who knew Catherine so well, tell us first what she was like at the age of ten:

> She had a thin, awkward figure, a sallow skin without colour, dark, lank hair and strong features... She was fond of all boys' plays, and greatly preferred cricket ... she had no taste for a garden... She was, moreover, noisy and wild, hated confinement and cleanliness, and *loved nothing so well in the world as rolling down the green slope at the back of the house.*

(Let us remember that in *A Memoir* J. E. Austen-Leigh mentions the green slope at the back of the house in Steventon and uses the above italicized words.)

Such was Catherine at ten. At fifteen, appearances were changing for the better: she began to curl her hair and to long to go to dances; her complexion improved; her features were softened by plumpness and colour, her eye gained animation. Her love for dirt gave way to an inclination for finery, and she grew clean as she grew smart. ' "Catherine grows quite a good-looking girl," ' sometimes her mother and father remarked. 'Her heart was affectionate, her disposition cheerful and open, without conceit or affectation of any kind ... her person pleasing, and when in good looks, pretty...' (*Northanger Abbey*, Penguin, 1987, p.41).

This was thus the young girl who accompanied Mr and Mrs Allen to spend six weeks in Bath. (In real life young Jane Austen had often visited Mrs Austen's cousins the Coopers and the Leigh-Perrots in Bath, getting to know the customs and the topography of the city — knowledge which she used in her novel *Northanger Abbey*.)

For the first time in her life Catherine Morland had the opportunity to spend a few weeks in Bath, to spend her first 'season' in a fashionable place. With an eager eye and keen mind she observed the social comedy around her. But the first days were rather dull. Mr and Mrs Allen knew nobody and Catherine had no partner to dance with.

Then, when the Allens and Catherine made their appearance one evening in the Lower Rooms the master of ceremonies introduced to Catherine 'a very gentleman-like young man, as a partner; his name was Tilney. He seemed to be about four or five and twenty, was rather tall, had a pleasing countenance, a very intelligent and lively eye, and if not quite handsome, was very near it. His address was good, and Catherine felt herself in high luck.'

While they were dancing there was little opportunity to talk. But when they were seated for tea, Catherine found him as agreeable as she had thought that he would be. He talked with fluency and had pleasant manners. With charming humour he made enquiries about her impressions of Bath, evoking the daily routine of the city: balls, concerts, theatre. She listened to him amused, not daring to laugh. He understood her hesitation:

> 'I see what you think of me,' he said gravely. 'I shall make but a poor figure in your journal to-morrow... Yes; I know exactly what you will say. Friday, went to the Lower Rooms; wore my sprigged muslin robe with blue trimmings — plain black shoes; appeared to much advantage, but was strangely harassed by a queer, half-witted man, who would make me dance with him, and distressed me by his nonsense.' — 'Indeed I shall not say such thing.' — 'Shall I tell you what you ought to say?' — 'If you please.' — 'I danced with a very agreeable young man, introduced by Mr King — had a great deal of conversation with him — seems a most extraordinary genius — hope I may know more of him. — *That*, madam, is what I *wish* you to say.'

Their conversation continued witty and pleasant on various subjects: on women keeping journals, on their easy style in writing letters. After a brief interruption, because of a short conversation between Mr Tilney and Mrs Allen, young Tilney tried to guess what Catherine was thinking:

> 'What are you thinking so earnestly?... not of your partner, I hope, for by that shake of the head your meditations are not satisfactory.' Catherine coloured, and said, 'I was not thinking of anything.' — 'That is artful and deep, to be sure; but I had rather be told at once that you will not tell me.' — 'Well, then, I will not.' — 'Thank you; for now we shall soon be acquainted, as I am authorized to tease you on this subject whenever we meet, and nothing in the world advances intimacy so much.'

It is a long quotation indeed — but it is worth one's while to underline it because it perhaps describes the first meeting between Jane Austen and Tom Lefroy and explains how their friendship and romance started. After this first encounter Catherine hoped to see her dancing partner again the following day. But days passed and he seemed to have vanished from Bath.

A small compensation for his absence was that Mrs Allen met an old school friend, Mrs Thorpe. Both were delighted to meet after many years. So Catherine was able with amusement to observe the ladies talking, but scarcely listening, to each other: 'in what they called conversation, but in which there was scarcely ever any exchange of opinion, and not often any resemblance of subject, for Mrs Thorpe talked chiefly of her children, and Mrs Allen of her gowns. (*Ibid.* p.57)

In the meantime a friendship began with Isabella the eldest daughter of Mrs Thorpe, a girl who was vain, silly and full of pretence. Her nonsensical talk often made Catherine blush. Listen to her:

> 'My attachments are always excessively strong ... The men think us incapable of real friendship ... Now, if I were to hear anybody speak slightingly of you, I should fire up in a moment; but that is not at all likely, for *you* are just the kind of girl to be a great favourite with the men.' — 'Oh dear!' cried Catherine, colouring; 'how can you say so?' — '...Oh! I must tell you that, just after we parted yesterday, I saw a young man looking at you so earnestly, I am sure he is in love with you.' Catherine coloured, and disclaimed again. (*Ibid.* pp.61–2)

Meeting Isabella's brother, John Thorpe, she listens politely to his vain chatter about horses, curricles, his gig:

> 'Do but look at my horse. Did you ever see an animal so made for speed in your life? ...look at his loins; only see how he moves; ... What do you think of my gig, Miss Morland? A neat one, is it not? Well hung; town built; I have not had it a month... Curricle-hung, you see; seat, trunk, sword-case, splashing-board, lamps, silver moulding, all, you see, complete...' (*Ibid.* pp.66–7)

In great contrast is Catherine's innocent, sincere behaviour. Asked if she is fond of an open carriage she answers spontaneously: ' "Yes, very. I have hardly ever had an opportunity of being in one; but I am particularly fond of it." '

At this first meeting, after talking about his horses, and his gig, John Thorpe, walking near to Catherine, now uttered no more than a short sentence of praise or condemnation of the face of every woman they met; and Catherine, after listening and agreeing as long as she could, with all the civility of a young woman's mind, ventured at length to vary the subject by a question which had long been uppermost in her thoughts; it was: ' "Have you ever read 'Udolpho', Mr Thorpe?" — " 'Udolpho'! Oh Lord! not I. I never read novels. I have something else to do." ' Later when he visits his mother young Thorpe greets her: ' "Ah, mother! how do you do? ...where did you get that quiz of a hat? It makes you look like an old witch." '

On his two younger sisters he bestowed equal portions of his fraternal tenderness; for he asked each of them how they did, and observed that they both looked very ugly. These manners did not please Catherine; but he was her brother's friend and Isabella's brother — and Isabella had assured her that John thought her the most charming girl in the world.

One evening Mr Tilney made his appearance in the Upper Rooms. He looked as handsome and lively as ever. Catherine, catching Mr Tilney's eye, instantly received from him a smile of recognition. She returned the smile with pleasure and then advancing towards him said: ' "I am very happy to see you again, sir, indeed; I was afraid you had left Bath." ' He thanked her for her fear and was charmed by her artless, cheerful sincerity. At the ball in the Upper

Rooms Catherine again had to listen to young Thorpe's uninteresting chatter about horses and dogs, and exchange of terriers.

On another evening Catherine met Isabella at the theatre. Let us reproduce once more Isabella's silly talk:

> 'Oh, heavens! my beloved Catherine, have I got you at last?... My sweetest Catherine, how have you been this long age? But I need not ask you, for you look delightfully. You really have done your hair in a more heavenly style than ever. You mischievous creature, do you want to attract everybody? I assure you my brother is quite in love with you already; and as for Mr Tilney — but *that* is a settled thing — even *your* modesty cannot doubt his attachment now... Oh! what would not I give to see him! I really am quite wild with impatience. My mother says he is the most delightful young man in the world;... you must introduce him to me. Is he in the house now? Look about for Heaven's sake! I assure you I can hardly exist till I see him.'
> (*Ibid.* p.89)

These are indeed extreme examples of mediocrity, of intellectual poverty, of lack of decency and kindness. In real life Jane Austen had of course met such persons though in her immediate surroundings she was blessed with kind-hearted, decent people, rising above mediocrity. Her father was a scholar, two of her brothers had studied in Oxford, others made honourable careers in the navy. Nevertheless, compared to the Thorpes, the Allens, the heroine and the hero of the novel, Catherine Morland and Henry Tilney, rise high above them all: Catherine with her charming personality made up of sincerity, modesty, tenderness of heart and wit and that of Henry a combination of intelligence, kindness, humour and a lively countenance.

If, as I suspect, it is her own story that Jane Austen is telling us, we can understand how wonderful it must have been for Jane and Tom to discover each other among hundreds of silly young girls and stupid young boys, in a desert of mediocrity and pretence. She was sparkling and he was shining. They recognized and highly valued each other. Theirs was not blind love. Their brilliant careers in later life were to confirm that what they saw and so loved in each other was true value, pure, unalloyed gold.

That Tom Lefroy was indeed a remarkable young man is confirmed by the following quotation from Park Honan's book:

> Tom Lefroy went to Trinity College Dublin. He was a dutiful boy, with such a 'kind disposition and affectionate heart' that his tutor Dr Burrowes took him into the Burrowes family circle. And when leaving College this same tutor said about him: 'No young man has left our College, with a higher character, so respected by all his Fellows... I can look with most assured confidence to his great advancement in life.' (*Jane Austen: Her Life*, Weidenfeld and Nicolson, 1987, pp.106–10)

But let us continue the novel. One Thursday evening Catherine was full of hope that Mr Tilney might ask her to dance. And indeed suddenly Mr Tilney stood before her and did ask her to dance. With sparkling eyes she granted his request. At this very moment a small incident occurred, a short conversation between young John Thorpe and Catherine. Mr Tilney protested:

> 'That gentleman would have put me out of patience, had he stayed with you half a minute longer. He has no business to withdraw the attention of my partner from me. We have entered into a contract of mutual agreeableness for the space of an evening, and all our agreeableness belongs solely to each other for that time. Nobody can fasten themselves on the notice of one without injuring the rights of the other. I consider a country-dance as an emblem of marriage. Fidelity and complaisance are the principal duties of both.'

This passage, with its reference to 'a contract of mutual agreeableness for the space of an evening', is very moving because of its flavour of authenticity. By evoking all the places in Bath which she knew so well: the Upper and Lower Rooms, the Pump Room, some special parts of the town: the Crescent, Milsom Street, Pulteney Street, the Pumpyard, the Archway opposite Union Passage — 'and how difficult it is to cross Cheap Street at this point' — it is as if Jane Austen was taking refuge in past and dear memories.

And let us meditate on the following paradox: in her first important novel — *Northanger Abbey* — containing autobiographical elements, the place where the plot starts is Bath; in *Persuasion*, which, as the last novel, has a deeper meaning than all her other novels, the happy reunion between Anne Elliot and Captain Wentworth occurs in Bath, which is again evoked with tenderness. These facts leave no doubt that this town was dear to Jane. Yet in spite of this, when she was told unexpectedly in 1801 that the family would move to Bath, Jane fainted. There is but one explanation: the place held too many dear and painful memories for her.

Young Jane Austen and Tom Lefroy must have spent happy days in Bath. Until recently this was but a supposition. In her old age Jane's sister, Cassandra Austen, destroyed much of their correspondence — chiefly Jane's letters of a personal nature. In what remains of Jane's letters we find all the same evidence of her having spent happy days in Bath with the Lefroy family. Here is the evidence in Letter 43, dated Monday 8 April 1805, to her sister Cassandra: 'This morning we have been to see Miss Chamberlayne look hot on horse back. Seven years and four months ago we went to the same Riding house to see Miss Lefroy's performances! — What a different set are we now in!' But knowing that her letter might be read by other members of the family Jane prudently added: 'But seven years are I suppose enough to change every pore of one's skin, and every feeling of one's mind.'

THE ROYAL CRESCENT, BATH

Reproduced from: *Bath and Bristol with the Counties of Somerset and Gloucester*, London 1829, by courtesy of the Rijksmuseum Stichting, Amsterdam.

Bath had a deep impact on Jane Austen's life — in times of joy, in times of sorrow. The whole meaning of this impact is still unknown...
'I really believe I shall always be talking of Bath, when I am home again — I *do* like it so very much... Oh, who can ever be tired of Bath?' (Jane Austen — *Northanger Abbey*). This was written in 1798.
'Tradition says that when Jane returned home ... the news was abruptly announced by her mother, who thus greeted them: "Well, girls, it is all settled; we have decided to leave Steventon in such a week, and go to Bath"; and that the shock of the intelligence was so great to Jane that she fainted away.' (*Life and Letters of Jane Austen* by William Austen-Leigh and Richard Arthur Austen-Leigh). This happened in 1801.
There is evidence that Jane Austen and Tom Lefroy were at the same time in Bath during the season in 1797. In a letter to her sister Cassandra dated 8 April 1805 Jane wrote: "This morning we have seen Miss Chamberlain look hot on horse back. Seven years and four months ago we went to the same Riding house to see Miss Lefroy's performances! — What a different set are we now in!" There is only one explanation for Jane to remember so well the year, the month — Tom Lefroy was also there... Those were the happy years...
'It will be two years to-morrow since we left Bath for Clifton, with what happy feelings of escape!' (Jane Austen — letter to her sister Cassandra, July 1808).

Today we may think that only if this memory of events which took place seven years earlier were connected with Tom Lefroy do these words of Jane's make sense.

In 1797 Jane had thus been in Bath at the same time as the Lefroy family. And Tom Lefroy's presence is the only reason why she should have remembered so precisely the year, the month. And indeed, in the Chronology at the end of R. W. Chapman's book *Jane Austen, Facts and Problems*, Oxford University Press, 1948, p.176, it is mentioned that in November 1797 'Cassandra E. and Jane Austen and mother with Leigh-Perrots at Paragon, Bath.'

(There must have been an important reason for Mrs Austen to decide to leave her favourite pastime, farming, and her beloved chicken house. And what might the reason have been if not to try to convince her brother Perrot to do something for Jane, in order to make the marriage with Tom Lefroy possible? But it seems that it all came to nothing and one might guess that it was Mrs Leigh-Perrot who opposed the liaison. This must have been the 'disappointment' which was talked about for many years in the Lefroy family — the discovery that after all the girl had nothing.)

These, then, were the happy days that Jane had spent in Bath with Tom Lefroy — when she loved Bath, and, like Catherine Morland, must have exclaimed: ' "I really believe I shall always be talking of Bath, when I am home again — I do like it so much... Oh, who can ever be tired of Bath?" ' (*Northanger Abbey*, Penguin, 1987, p.97)

And only the events that were to separate the young people for ever can explain the change in Jane's feelings for that town. For Jane felt a great relief when, with her mother and sister, they left Bath in 1806. In a letter to Cassandra (Letter 54, dated 30 June 1808) she wrote: 'It will be two years to-morrow since we left Bath for Clifton, with what happy feelings of escape!'

Let us now continue the thread of the novel. This 'contract of mutual agreeableness' must have marked a turning point in their relationship and was a mark of Henry Tilney's recognition and appreciation of Catherine's special qualities.

On that special evening they go on talking about more serious things. About how she likes Bath or prefers to live in the country, comparing both. He is charmed by Catherine's enthusiasm, and when she exclaims: ' "Who can ever be tired of Bath?" ' his answer is: ' "Not those who bring such fresh feelings of every sort to it, as you do." ' At the end of the evening, before parting from Mr Tilney, his sister and Catherine decide to take a walk together in the country the next day.

Let us at this point mention an interesting coincidence: in the novel it is stated that 'Miss Tilney always wears white.' (*Northanger Abbey*, Penguin, 1987, p.107) And Jane's Irish friend, Tom Lefroy 'a very gentleman-like, good-looking, pleasant young man ... has but one fault ... it is that his morning coat is a great deal too light...' (Letter, to Cassandra, dated January 1796) 'I look forward with great impatience, to our party at Ashe to-morrow night as I rather expect to receive an offer from my friend in the course of the evening. I shall refuse him, however, unless he promises to give up his white coat.' (Letter 2, to Cassandra, dated 14 January, 1796)

It is evident that we have here a mirror image of what occurred in real life, where it was not a young girl who always wore white but a young man.

At this stage of their relationship Henry Tilney's father — General Tilney, who was also in Bath — approves the growing friendship between his two children and Miss Catherine Morland, believing her to be a rich heiress. Among other evidence of his approval, the General admired: 'the elasticity of her walk, which corresponded exactly with the spirit of her dancing...' Reading these words we have to think of what her nephew J. E. Austen-Leigh wrote in his *Memoir*, pointing to the fact that Jane had a particular way of walking, which caught the attention, for after many years he writes: 'Her figure was rather slender, her step light and firm, and her whole appearance expressive of health and animation.' (A *Memoir*, 1869, Penguin, 1986, p.330)

Let us also mention what another member of the Lefroy family thought of young Jane Austen. It is Sir Egerton Brydges, brother of Mrs Lefroy: both of them were to play an important part in the breaking of the romance between Jane and Tom Lefroy. In his *The Autobiography* he writes: 'My eye told me that she was fair and handsome, slight and elegant.'

These different testimonies in the novel and from real life differ only in words, but they express the same idea of health, liveliness and elegance. On different occasions Catherine and Henry Tilney talk, getting to know each other still better. When they talk about novels Catherine is very pleased to hear that he enjoys reading them. Henry thinks that: ' "The person, be it gentleman or lady, who has not pleasure in a good novel must be intolerably stupid." '

We come to know that both young Tilneys, brother and sister, are fond of history. (It is certain that, as a graduate in law, young Tom Lefroy was interested in history and politics. When he was a student at Trinity College, Dublin, he was an active and enthusiastic member of the Historical Society.) Catherine also reckons that her father and brothers are fond of history. Their discussion is amusing: Catherine thinks that books of history are written to *torment* small children, while Henry uses the phrase *to instruct*.

These discussions took place during a country walk around Bath, to the top of Beechen Cliff. At the end of the walk Catherine was invited for dinner with the Tilneys for the day after the next. Her only difficulty was 'in concealing the excess of her pleasure'.

Let us mention what Catherine said during a conversation with Isabella about fortune and marriage: ' "I hate the idea of one fortune looking for another." ' This passage acquires a deeper meaning when we think that the principal reason which put an end to Jane Austen's relationship with Tom Lefroy was her poverty and that the young man himself was not deprived of means. On the contrary, he was the protégé of his wealthy great-uncle Benjamin Langlois who had great projects for his nephew. *He* was not to be disappointed by a marriage to an inferior partner. Tom Lefroy's marriage was thus to be a question of prestige, of 'one fortune looking for another'.

The friendship between Catherine and Henry makes further progress. They talk and dance and Catherine 'enjoyed her usual happiness with Henry, listening with sparkling eyes to everything he said; and, in finding him irresistible, becoming so herself'.

One evening an event occurs which Catherine attributes to the good nature of the person implied. Henry Tilney is very impressed:

> '...your attributing my brother's wish of dancing with Miss Thorpe to good-nature alone, convinced me of your being superior in good-nature yourself to all the rest of the world.' Catherine blushed and disclaimed, and the gentleman's predictions were verified. There was a something, however, in his words ... that occupied her mind so much that she drew back for some time, forgetting to speak or to listen, and almost forgetting where she was... (*Northanger Abbey*, p.142)

Mutual discovery of those precious qualities of the heart brings them closer and closer.

A most pleasant surprise awaits Catherine: General Tilney invites her to be their guest at Northanger Abbey. She is elated to rapture: 'to be their chosen visitor, she was to be for weeks under the same roof with the person whose society she mostly prized...' (*Ibid.* p.149)

One evening Catherine and Henry are discussing Isabella's behaviour towards the man she is engaged to and Henry makes a wise remark: ' "No man is offended by another man's admiration of the woman he loves; it is the woman only who can make it a torment." '

The journey to Northanger Abbey starts after a breakfast in Milsom Street. Miss Tilney is friendly and Henry's smile makes Catherine feel comfortable. But the excessive attentions of General Tilney make her uneasy. They all leave Bath — the two girls and a maid in a carriage and four, General Tilney and Henry in a curricle.

After a two hours' wait before continuing the journey, General Tilney proposes to Catherine that she takes a place in his son's curricle:

> in the course of a few minutes she found herself with Henry in the curricle, as happy a being as ever existed... Henry drove so well, so quietly, without making any disturbance, without parading to her, or swearing [at the horses] ... And then his hat sat so well, and the innumerable capes of his great-coat looked so becomingly important! To be driven by him, next to being dancing with him, was certainly the greatest happiness in the world. (*Ibid.* p.163)

In the novel — from chapter 21 — follows a detailed description of Catherine Morland's visit to Northanger Abbey and the adventures she has, inspired by her romantic reading. We shall ignore all that caught the eye and interest of previous readers and critics who saw in this novel 'the adventures of a charmingly imperfect heroine who meets all the trappings of Gothic horror and imagines the worst'.

We shall continue to mention only the various circumstances marking the progress of Catherine's and Henry's relationship, and also those events which may have happened in real life when this seems to be the only reason why they are mentioned, or because they throw light on the heroes' characters — as, for example, General Tilney's strict punctuality: 'Catherine found herself hurried away by Miss Tilney in such a manner as convinced her that the strictest punctuality to the family hours would be expected at Northanger.' (Ibid. p.168)

We may ask ourselves: 'Was the strictest punctuality also a rule at Ashe where Jane often visited the Lefroy family?'

And Catherine's sudden love for hyacinths (Ibid. p.178) — Miss Tilney just taught her to love this flower. Henry Tilney does appreciate her capacity for learning: ' "I am pleased that you have learned to love a hyacinth. The mere habit of learning to love is the thing; and a teachableness of disposition in a young lady is a great blessing." ' (Ibid. p.179) On this occasion we again see Henry's wisdom when he praises her new love for the hyacinth: ' "You have gained a new source of enjoyment, and it is well to have as many holds upon happiness as possible." '

General Tilney himself offers to show Northanger Abbey to his young visitor: first the garden and the shrubberies. The kitchen garden was next to be admired. The number of acres contained in this garden was such that Catherine 'could not listen to without dismay ... The general was flattered by her looks of surprise, which told him ... that she had never seen any gardens at all equal to them before ... If he had a hobby-horse, it was that. He loved a garden.' (Ibid. p.182)

It is evident that he shows to Catherine all the beauty and grandeur of his property as to a future daughter-in-law.

During many a conversation with the young Tilneys Catherine found, with a little surprise, that wealth was very important for the General when it came to family connections, marriage and so on — and some alarm, for 'She was as insignificant and perhaps as portionless as Isabella...'

One day, General Tilney proposed to visit Henry in his own home. Henry was honoured and very happy and Catherine was delighted with the scheme. The visit was a success. There is little doubt that all these small events would soon lead to a more important one: the engagement between Catherine and Henry.

After a few days the General was obliged to go to London. The two girls spend some quiet pleasant days together. Catherine almost always believed that Henry loved her. An appointment with his curate at Woodston obliged him to leave the girls for a couple of days.

It was in the evening of the day that Henry had left Northanger Abbey that General Tilney returned unexpectedly. But not only was his return unexpected.

The complete change of his attitude towards Catherine worried and frightened Eleanor Tilney. Without any explanation he ordered Catherine's immediate departure from Northanger Abbey. Catherine was deprived of any possibility of choosing for herself the day and hour which would be convenient for her to give her time to announce to her parents her impending arrival. General Tilney had arranged everything; a carriage early in the morning next day was to take her away. Miss Tilney was very distressed at having to announce to her friend the General's decision:

> 'Ah Catherine ... how can I tell you? — to-morrow morning is fixed for your leaving us, and not even the hour is left to your choice; the very carriage is ordered, and will be here at seven o'clock, and no servant will be offered you... Good God! what will your father and mother say? ... to have you driven out of the house, without the considerations even of decent civility!' (Ibid. p.223)

Catherine was speechless when listening to Eleanor's message. She is assaulted by a hundred thoughts — had she offended the General? Her friend also tried to find an explanation: ' "His temper is not happy ... some disappointment, some vexation, which just at this moment seems important, but which I can hardly suppose you to have any concern in, for how is it possible?" ' Once alone Catherine gave way to her distress:

> Turned from the house, and in such a way, without any reason that could justify, any apology that could atone for the abruptness, the rudeness, nay, the insolence of it. Henry at a distance — not able even to bid him farewell. Every hope, every expectation from him suspended, at least, and who could say how long? Who could say when they might meet again? ... The manner in which it was done so grossly uncivil: *hurrying her away without any reference to her own convenience...* (Ibid. p.224) (Author's italics)

And at these very words, 'hurrying her away', I stopped abruptly — for also in real life somebody had been hurried away. While reading I was eagerly looking for a circumstance, an event which might recall an event or circumstance from real life, and there it was indeed! Except that in real life it was not *a girl* who had been hurried away but *a young man*.

But let us recapitulate and explain. As stated in the Introduction to *Northanger Abbey* by Ann E. Ehrenpreis, the plot in the novel 'was originally concerned with a young girl's entrance into the world'. It was to that plot that Jane Austen added the Gothic passages, probably as a diversion from the plot which was too autobiographical. The result was that 'most critics agree that the Gothic burlesque is not well blended with the rest of the story'. (Introduction to *Northanger Abbey*, by Ann E. Ehrenpreis, Penguin, 1987, p.13)

The important story that Jane Austen tried to tell is of the special encounter between two very gifted, brilliant young people. Their intellectual and spiritual qualities placed them high above the average. Sympathy, admiration and friendship would lead them to love: for one of them a long lasting love. Their love story was to be ended abruptly by material considerations. The end of the real story is the mirror image of what is told in the novel. It was not a man who hurried away a young girl, but a lady who hurried away a young man in order to prevent mischief.

Many years later, in 1869, Tom Lefroy's sister Caroline wrote in a letter: 'It was a disappointment, but Mrs Lefroy sent the gentleman off ... that no more mischief might be done.' Mischief, meaning that young Tom Lefroy should propose to a girl deprived of fortune, Jane Austen.

The speed of sending off — of hurrying away Tom Lefroy — is mentioned twice in Park Honan's book: 'In alarm, Mrs Lefroy made Tom leave Hampshire as soon as possible.' (*Jane Austen: Her Life*, by Park Honan, Weidenfeld and Nicolson, 1987, p.110) And: 'Alarmed by Jane Austen's flirtation with her husband's nephew Tom Lefroy, Anne sent the young man off in a hurry.' (*Ibid.* pp.212-13)

It is interesting to remember that Jane Austen's mother was a Leigh of Adlestrop in Gloucestershire; a younger, but ennobled, branch of the same family is Leigh of Stoneleigh in Warwickshire. Cassandra's grandfather had married a Brydges, and so became brother-in-law to the Duke of Chandos. Mrs Austen was connected with the academic clergy of Oxford and had a pedigree. One uncle was Theophilus Leigh, Master of Balliol. Her father Thomas Leigh, was a fellow of All Souls. Through her mother Jane thus had aristocratic connections. And being the niece of the 'wealthy and childless' Leigh-Perrots she could have given the impression of being herself a possible heiress.

We should also remember that Bath's beauty and glitter was in part owed to Mrs Austen's own great-uncle, the Duke of Chandos, who, as the Perrots had always been proud to say, had places in the town named after him.

In 1719 James Brydges had been created first Duke of Chandos. A few years later he visited Bath, which at that time was a forlorn town victimized by gamblers, pickpockets and sedan-chairmen. Yet it had a vogue as a watering place since Roman times.

Chandos sensed a real potential in this town, invested in development and hired an architect surveyor: he was John Wood, a self-trained mythologist and an ambitious visionary inspired by the precedents of Greece and Rome. So began the road to Bath's glory and grandeur.

To Mrs Anne Lefroy and her brother Sir Egerton Brydges, so fond of heraldry and aristocratic genealogy, these genealogical details of the Austen family must have been well known. Their only mistake was to believe that material advantages were associated with these aristocratic connections.

Perhaps this is the right place to say something about what some wealthy relatives could have done for Jane. For the rich Perrots it would have been but a small sacrifice to assure for Jane an income which would have made her an eligible young girl. Like her heroine, Elizabeth Bennet, young Jane was made for happiness — and her marriage with Tom Lefroy would then have been possible.

No doubt the move to Bath was inspired in Rev. George Austen by the hope that his wealthy brother-in-law would do something for his daughters, by the hope that living in the same town would bring them nearer and that out of reciprocal sympathy a positive result might be obtained. The generous offer to send his daughters to keep Mrs Leigh-Perrot company in jail must also have been inspired by a similar hope. But one has only to look at Mrs Leigh-Perrot's portrait, at her moroseness and her expressionless eyes, and it becomes evident that no bond could have existed between her and her witty and lively niece!

In the novel, Mr and Mrs Allen, with whom Catherine Morland stayed in Bath, were also rich and childless, which made young Thorpe believe that Catherine was a rich heiress. He questioned her about the Allens, about their fortune, and in consequence paid assiduous attention to Catherine.

Sir Egerton Brydges and his sister Mrs Lefroy, for whom connections and fortune were of great importance, might have believed Jane Austen to have them both. This explains the growing intimacy that was permitted, and which lasted at least two years, between Tom Lefroy and Jane. And when, after enquiries, they discovered the truth, they decided to make an abrupt end to the relationship.

As in real life the explanation in the novel of General Tilney's behaviour was his discovery that Miss Catherine Morland was not the rich heiress he had believed her to be!

It was this story that young Jane wrote in her grief during the difficult year after their abrupt separation, taking refuge in cherished memories.

It is now generally agreed that *Pride and Prejudice* was conceived in 1797 when, as we now know, hope and dreams of happiness were still possible. They are reflected in this novel in which Jane Austen reached summits of sparkling wit and carefree joy which she would never reach again in her later novels. Other summits she would attain — but never would she be again able to express the carefree happiness of Elizabeth Bennet.

Elizabeth Jenkins was aware of the unique brilliance of *Pride and Prejudice*: 'The celestial brightness of *Pride and Prejudice* is unequalled even in Jane Austen's other work ... the whole field of the novel glitters as with sunrise upon morning dew. The impression cannot wholly be analysed and accounted for.' (Elizabeth Jenkins, *Jane Austen, A Biography*, Victor Gollancz Ltd, London. 1938, p.196)

It was in 1797 that Mrs Austen wrote to her future daughter-in-law Mary Lloyd: 'I look forward to you as a real comfort to me in old age when Cassandra is gone into Shropshire, and Jane — the Lord knows where...' (We may fill in: 'the Lord knows where ... in Ireland.')

We know also that *Northanger Abbey* was written in 1798, after Jane had herself had the experience of somebody being 'hurried away' in order to prevent a 'low' marriage, though in 1798 there still was hope, as the tone of some of her letters show.

In *A Memoir* J. E. Austen-Leigh evokes that love story with the following sentences:

> At Ashe also, Jane became acquainted with a member of the Lefroy family, who was still living when I began these memoirs, a few months ago: the Right Hon. Thomas Lefroy, late Chief Justice of Ireland. One must look back more than seventy years to reach the time when these two bright young persons were, for a short time, intimately acquainted with each other, and then separated on their several courses, never to meet again; both destined to attain some distinction in their different ways, one to survive the other for more than half a century, yet in his extreme old age to remember and speak, as he sometimes did, of his former companion, as one to be much admired, and not easily forgotten by those who had ever known her. (*A Memoir*, 1869, Penguin, 1986, pp.309–10)

II PERSUASION — WHAT JANE AUSTEN WISHED TO TELL IN HER LAST NOVEL

To the memory of Mia Gerhard who enabled me to connect three of the greatest among the great — Shakespeare, Jane Austen and Marcel Proust — this chapter is dedicated.

'When to the sessions of sweet silent thought I summon up remembrance of things past...' — Shakespeare, *Sonnets*

Jane Austen's last novel, *Persuasion*, is considered 'her most poignant and personal fiction, not because she died soon after writing it, but because of what it contains... It has provoked considerable biographical speculation.' (Robert K. Wallace: *Jane Austen and Mozart — Classical Equilibrium in Fiction and Music*, The University of Georgia Press, Athens, 1983, pp.189, 236)

Reading *Persuasion* for the second time immediately after *Northanger Abbey* increased in my mind the certitude that it is also an autobiographical story: that the author — perhaps with a presentiment that this would be her last book — returned after twenty years to the most important event of her life: her short but intense relationship with Tom Lefroy.

Like *Northanger Abbey*, her first important novel, *Persuasion* tells about 'love threatened by interference'. In *Northanger Abbey* a young girl is 'hurried away' to prevent her lover proposing to her because she is too insignificant — she has no money and no connections.

In *Persuasion* a young girl is 'persuaded' to break her engagement with a young man because he is too insignificant. The knowledge we have of Jane Austen's life enables us to understand that these are mirror images of what happened in real life: the young man — Tom Lefroy — was 'persuaded' and 'sent off' in order to prevent him from marrying a poor girl.

In *Persuasion* at the very core of the novel is Anne Elliot's long-lasting love for Frederick Wentworth. Love and constancy were also to be Jane's part. The happy ending belongs only in fiction. The many autobiographical details and circumstances which we recognize in the novel give it an extra moving dimension.

Let us from the start point to the fact that only in these two novels —

Northanger Abbey and Persuasion — the background is a real place, Bath, while in all her other novels the characters are placed in imaginary towns and villages. Often details mentioned in Persuasion resemble details from Northanger Abbey or recall facts from real life. Whenever these resemblances occur, I shall mention them as a proof of their authenticity.

I propose to mention and analyse them in chronological order. In chapter four of Persuasion the hero and heroine are introduced to the reader: Frederick Wentworth as he was in his youth 'a remarkably fine young man, with a great deal of intelligence, spirit and brilliancy; and Anne an extremely pretty girl, with gentleness, modesty, taste and feeling'.

In Northanger Abbey young Tilney is described as a young man 'rather tall, had a pleasing countenance, a very intelligent and lively eye, and if not quite handsome, was very near it.' (Northanger Abbey, Penguin, 1987, p.47)

On page 41 of Northanger Abbey Catherine Morland is introduced: 'her heart was affectionate, her disposition cheerful and open, without conceit or affectation of any kind ... her person pleasing, and, when in good looks, pretty.'

It is evident that, though with different words and an interval of twenty years, the same two charming personalities are evoked. These two young people meet, become gradually acquainted 'and when acquainted, rapidly and deeply, in love'. (Persuasion, Penguin, 1986, p.55)

It might be interesting to remember that the same *accord parfait* right from the start also occurs in Northanger Abbey when at their very first meeting at a ball in Bath Henry Tilney says to Catherine: ' "now we shall soon be acquainted, as I am authorized to tease you on this subject whenever we meet, and nothing in the world advances intimacy so much." ' (Northanger Abbey, Penguin, 1987, p.51)

The spark of sympathy and interest is already there! It should also be noted that in no other of Jane Austen's novels does the *accord parfait* occur so rapidly. In Sense and Sensibility it takes quite a time before Marianne Dashwood finds happiness with Colonel Brandon. Only after many tribulations are Elizabeth Bennet and Darcy happily united; Emma Woodhouse needs many years to discover that she loves Mr Knightley, and Fanny Price has to wait in anguish and uncertainty for the affection of her cousin Edmund Bertram.

It is also interesting to mention Lady Russell's reasoning. Being an affectionate friend of Anne's she thought so highly of Anne's qualities that she considered an alliance with a young man deprived of fortune and connections a most unfortunate one:

> Anne Elliot, so young; known to so few, to be snatched off by a stranger without alliance or fortune; or rather sunk by him into a state of most wearing, anxious, youth-killing dependance! It must not be, if by any fair interference of friendship ... it would be prevented. (Persuasion, Penguin, 1986, p.56)

These might have been the very thoughts, even the very words, thought and pronounced by Mrs Lefroy, the aunt of young Tom Lefroy and a friend of Jane Austen. Thus must she have argued and explained to both young people — and in the end she 'persuaded' her nephew and 'sent him off' in order to prevent more mischief.

As in real life, Anne Elliot's romance with Frederick Wentworth lasted but a short time — 'it lasted a short period of exquisite felicity.' Their acquaintance was soon ended and for Anne (as for Jane) 'not with a few months ended Anne's share of suffering from it. Her attachment and regrets had, for a long time, clouded every enjoyment of youth; and an early loss of bloom and spirits had been their lasting effect.' (Ibid. p.57)

Very early a place was mentioned which was to play an important role in the novel. It is Bath, first mentioned in connection with Sir Walter Elliot and his two daughters moving to that town. We should bear in mind that it was in Bath that Catherine Morland first met Henry Tilney, that the street in Bath in which General Tilney, his son and daughter took lodgings — Milsom Street — was the same street in which a most important event in *Persuasion* occurred.

Various streets and places in Bath are so frequently recalled that even the reader who has never visited this town gets the impression that he knows it and loves it. There is no doubt that in real life Bath was associated for Jane with sweet and painful memories.

At page 61 of *Persuasion* are mentioned 'the heats of September in all the white glare of Bath' — evoking as if in a dream the elegant sparkling white buildings of the town.

It was decided that Anne would join her father and sister in Bath only after they were settled in the new apartment. In the meantime she would go to cheer up her sister Mary and keep her company at Uppercross. Anne left her father's house, Kellynch Hall, on the same day as the rest of the family, 'and Anne walked up at the same time, in a sort of desolate tranquillity ... It was painful to look upon their deserted grounds, and still worse to anticipate the new hands they were to fall into.'

Once at Uppercross Anne told her sister how busy she had been before leaving Kellynch Hall, and that she had had to do:

> 'A great many things ... More than I can recollect in a moment ... I have been making a duplicate of the catalogue of my father's books and pictures. I have been several times in the garden with Mackenzie, trying to understand, and make him understand, which of Elizabeth's plants are for Lady Russell. I have had all my own little concerns to arrange — books and music to divide, and all my trunks to repack ... And one thing ... of a more trying nature; going to almost every house in the parish, as a sort of take-leave. I was told that they wished it.' (Ibid. p.66)

It is a moving passage, doubtless autobiographical, evoking young Jane at the time when the Austen family was leaving Steventon, in order to move to Bath, in 1801.

Let us for a moment turn aside from the novel and consider Jane Austen's attitude towards dancing. In R. W. Chapman's book *Jane Austen, Facts and Problems* a general view is given of how her attitude towards dancing changed through the years. It is an impressive selection of letters evoking first young Jane as a passionate dancer. Here is a passage from one of her letters:

> There were twenty dances, and I danced them all and without fatigue. I was glad to find myself capable of dancing so much, and with so much satisfaction as I did ... I had not thought myself equal to it, but in cold weather and with a few couples I fancy I could just as well dance for a week together... (Letter to Cassandra, dated 24 XII, 1798)

Those were the happy years — dancing in real life, and dancing in fiction, country dances with a young man who considered them as an emblem of marriage. But there were to come years, in fiction as in real life, when the joy of dancing would fade and Jane, still young and pretty, would prefer to sit at the pianoforte, playing while the others danced. In later years her letters evoked the even quieter pleasure of sitting near the open hearth with a glass of wine and watching the dancing.

In *Persuasion*, Anne, the heroine, had given up dancing. She prefers to play the pianoforte for others. While Anne was staying at Uppercross with her sister Mary, they often visited the Great House, the home of the Musgrove family. The Musgrove girls were wild about dancing; and evenings ended, occasionally, in an unpredictable little ball: '[friends, members of the family] would come at any time, and help play at any thing, or dance any where; and Anne, very much preferring the office of musician to a more active post, played country dances to them by the hour together...' (*Persuasion*, Penguin, 1986, p.73)

There can be no doubt that young Jane, in the years that followed Tom Lefroy's departure, when her joy in dancing had vanished, while she was playing country dances for others was thinking of what a young man had once said about them.

During her visits at Uppercross Anne had to listen to many small complaints from different members of the family — from her sister Mary, from Mary's husband Charles, from Mrs Musgrove — trying to understand everybody, giving advice, always patient, always kind. Very often they complained to her about each other: 'How was Anne to set all these matters to rights? She could do little more than listen patiently, soften every grievance, and excuse each to the other, give them all hints of the forbearance necessary between such close neighbours...' (*Ibid.* p.72)

This passage evokes circumstances from real life that must often have occurred when Jane Austen visited members of her large family. In *A Memoir* her nephew J. E. Austen-Leigh writes:

> I have recollected some of the bright qualities which shone, as it were, on the surface of Jane Austen's character, and attracted most notice; but underneath them, there lay the strong foundations of sound sense and judgement, rectitude of principle, and delicacy of feeling, qualifying her equally to advise, assist, or amuse. She was, in fact, as ready to comfort the unhappy, or to nurse the sick, as she was to laugh and jest with the light-hearted. (A *Memoir*, 1869, Penguin, 1986, p.338)

In *Persuasion*, unlike in real life, the hero reappears. And very often descriptions are given of his manners, general appearance and countenance. A few weeks after Anne's arrival at Uppercross, Captain Wentworth paid a visit to Mr and Mrs Musgrove at the Great House. It was from the two Musgrove girls, Louisa and Henrietta, that Anne heard words full of praise about him.

> [The girls had been] perfectly delighted ... with him, how much handsomer, how infinitely more agreeable they thought him than any individual among their male acquaintance ... how glad they had been ... when he had promised in reply to papa and mamma's ... pressing invitations, to come and dine with them on the morrow ... And he had promised it in so pleasant a manner ... And, in short, he had looked and said every thing with such exquisite grace, that they could assure them all, their heads were both turned by him! (*Persuasion*, Penguin, 1986, p.80)

In David Cecil's book: *A Portrait of Jane Austen* a portrait of young Tom Lefroy is reproduced. He was indeed a very handsome young man — with a regular face, a lively eye and a sweet smile. Looking at the portrait one can understand the deep and lasting affection which Jane cherished for him.

A short time after Captain Wentworth's arrival at Uppercross an encounter between him and Anne took place. It was a very short social meeting. His comment on her afterwards, reported to Anne by Henrietta was: ' "he said you were so altered he should not have known you." ' For Anne his words proved that he had not forgiven her. 'She had used him ill; deserted and disappointed him; and worse, she had shewn a feebleness of character in doing so, which his own decided, confident temper could not endure... It had been the effect of over-persuasion. It had been weakness and timidity.' (*Ibid.* p.86)

A very interesting passage because *mutatis mutandis* it is the very judgement that Jane Austen might have applied and in fact did apply to young Tom Lefroy. He was deeply in love with her, on the point of being engaged — had they been engaged? — and allowed himself to be persuaded, over-persuaded, to give her up. Had the charming personality of Tom Lefroy some flaws? Were they the very ones mentioned by Anne Elliot: feebleness of character, weakness, timidity?

It is also interesting to mention the description that Captain Wentworth gave of the woman he would choose as his wife: she should have: ' "A strong mind, with sweetness of manner." ': a most rare and precious combination. Anne Elliot had been such a woman. And after reading in A Memoir the witness of her nephew 'that there was scarcely a charm in her most delightful characters that was not a true reflection of her own sweet temper and loving heart' we know that, like Anne Elliot, Jane Austen had possessed these qualities that Tom Lefroy had loved and appreciated.

In the twentieth century it is perhaps difficult to understand that he gave her up. But two hundred years ago, and even more recently than that, the mentality was different — life was considered a serious matter and important things were not to be sacrificed for 'youthful love'.

In Caroline Austen's *Reminiscences* the general opinion about 'romantic youthful love' is expressed. Writing about two people in love, she writes: 'The love to which I have referred, though sincere and strong, I believe on both sides, was not of that romantic, youthful nature, which foresees no evil in poverty and in the change of social position that is sure to follow.' (*Reminiscences of Caroline Austen*, The Jane Austen Society, 1986, p.28)

One day Anne, her sister Mary, the two Musgrove girls and Captain Wentworth take a long walk. Anne pauses to rest on a bank and listens unwillingly to a discussion between Louisa Musgrove and Frederick Wentworth. He is pleading for fortitude and strength of mind: ' "It is the worst evil of too yielding and indecisive a character... You are never sure of a good impression being durable. Every body may sway it; let those who would be happy be firm ... My first wish for all, whom I am interested in, is that they should be firm." ' (*Persuasion*, Penguin, 1986, p.110)

Should we not conclude that these words express what Jane Austen was thinking — after twenty years — of the friend she had dearly loved and still loved? He had lacked fortitude and strength of mind, the strong impression she had made upon him had not been durable; his character had been too yielding and indecisive. 'And his having a warm and amiable heart' made the loss even greater.

From chapter 13 the setting of the novel is in Bath. Before we enter Anne Elliot's Bath period let us stop and try to analyse what this town had meant in real life to Jane Austen.

Connecting everything with everything — the shock Jane felt when she was told that the family would move to Bath, the fact that she almost stopped writing during the years she lived there — we may conclude that the Bath period had been a very painful one for Jane. There is little doubt that there was grief after Tom Lefroy's departure and that in that town she was confronted with memories of happy days.

All these feelings must have had an influence on her countenance. Like Anne Elliot in the novel, Jane must have become another woman. Her cheerfulness, her playful mind were tempered. These changes must also have been noticed by others. An explanation had to be found for the 'world' — and it was found. It is at this period that the 'family tale' has it that at a seaside resort — Sidmouth — Jane met 'the young man whom she might one day have married. Tragically he died quite suddenly afterwards...'

The sad aftermath of this Devonshire holiday was a safe and honourable explanation for Jane's change of countenance. It was a story one could tell to the 'world' without loss of face. It seems that Tom Lefroy's conduct towards Jane must have been considered by the Austen family as most outrageous, and as a grave offence against the whole family. In consequence they did all that was possible to hide Jane's suffering.

The resentment against the Lefroy family was to survive for many years. That relations between the two families were cool might be proved by the most strange and gloomy atmosphere which prevailed at a family event which took place nearly twenty years later.

On 8 November 1814 Anna, the eldest daughter of James Austen and one of Jane's favourite nieces, was married to Benjamin Lefroy. Anna's half-sister Caroline was then nine years old. Here are her reminiscences of that day:

> My sister's wedding was certainly in the extreme of quietness... The season of the year, the unfrequented road to the church, the grey light within ... no stove to give warmth, no flowers to give colour and brightness, no friends, high or low, to offer their good wishes, and so to claim some interest in the great event of the day — all these circumstances and deficiencies must, I think, have given a gloomy air to the wedding... Nor was anyone asked to the breakfast, to which we sat down as soon as we got back ... Soon after the breakfast the bride and bridegroom departed. (*Reminiscences of Caroline Austen*, The Jane Austen Society, 1986, p.40)

A most strange wedding indeed, in a family of seven children — five sons and two daughters. James Austen was the oldest brother. All the brothers and sisters loved each other dearly and entertained a lively relationship, visiting each other very often. Was it a silent opposition to that marriage? Were old griefs and painful memories still strongly felt? It seems that the engagement between the two young people had caused 'consternation' in the Austen family. There is one more proof that there might have been serious reasons for bitterness and resentment: fifty years later there was somebody who remembered what had happened between young Jane Austen and Tom Lefroy and who tried to excuse the latter. It was Tom Lefroy's sister Caroline who, in a letter wrote the following, (with some *heat* as R. W. Chapman underlines, though fifty years had passed):

> I think I need not warn *you* against raking up that old story of the still living Chief Justice (Tom Lefroy). That there was something in it, is true ... but nothing to call ill usage, and no very serious sorrow endured. The York Lefroys got up a very strong version of it all, and spread their own notions

to the family — but they were for years very angry with their kinsman, and rather delighted in a proof as they thought, of his early heartlessness. I have *my* story from my mother, who was near at the time. It was a disappointment ... but there was *no* engagement, and never *had* been.
(quoted by R. W. Chapman in *Jane Austen, Facts and Problems*, Oxford University Press, 1948, pp.57–8)

To this statement we may oppose a passage from one of Jane's early letters (Letter 2, to Cassandra, dated 14 January 1796) in which we read: 'Our party at Ashe to-morrow night ... I look forward with great impatience to it, as I rather expect to receive an offer from my friend in the course of the evening. I shall refuse him, however, unless he promises to give away his white coat.'

This letter was followed by a silence which lasted until August 1796 — and then by a long silence until November 1798. It is indeed a subject for meditation and wonder. It is also interesting to consider a letter that Anna Lefroy (*née* Austen) whose wedding Caroline so well remembered, wrote to Emma Austen-Leigh at the time when James Edward was gathering information for the *Memoir* about his aunt. In this letter Anna recollected what she had heard about Jane's relationship with Tom Lefroy.

> When I came to hear again and again, from those who were old enough to remember, how the Mother had disliked Tom Lefroy because he had behaved so ill to Jane Austen, with sometimes additional weight of the Father's condemnation, what could I think *then*? ... The one thing certain is, that to the last year of his life she was remembered as the object of his youthful admiration — they were within a short month of the same age.
> (Deirdre Le Faye, *Tom Lefroy and Jane Austen*, Report of the Jane Austen Society, 1985)

The letter was written on May 24 1869, and lifts a corner of the veil of mystery that surrounded the whole affair. In any case this fragment proves that things had been more serious than the Austen family wanted the world to believe.

With all these things in mind Jane wrote her last novel. With these same things in mind, let us follow Anne Elliot to Bath, where a new period of her life was to begin.

Anne leaves Uppercross after Louisa Musgrove's accident in Lyme and goes to join her father and sister in Bath. Their new lodging is in Camden Place and Sir Walter Elliot and Elizabeth are very proud of their new home. From now on, places and streets in Bath are mentioned and described very frequently. It is in the company of Lady Russell that Anne comes to Bath 'on a wet afternoon, and driving through the long course of streets from the Old Bridge to Camden-place, amidst the dash of other carriages, the heavy rumble of carts and drays, the bawling of newsmen, muffin-men and milk-men, and the ceaseless clink of

CAMDEN PLACE, BATH

Reproduced from: *Bath and Bristol with the Counties of Somerset and Gloucester*, London 1829, by courtesy of the Rijksmuseum Stichting, Amsterdam.

pattens'. Lady Russell thought that 'these were noises which belonged to the winter pleasures'.

In mentioning Anne's disinclination for Bath we may presume that Jane attributes to her heroine her own dislike for a town associated with many happy and painful memories.

Friends of Sir Walter Elliot are living in Marlborough Buildings in very good style. Standing in a shop in Bond Street, Sir Walter Elliot 'had counted eighty-seven women go by, one after another, without there being a tolerable face among them'. (Like young Thorpe in *Northanger Abbey*.) One evening, on his way home from a dinner in Lansdown Crescent, Mr Elliot stopped at Sir Walter Elliot's to enquire if all were well.

In the Bath paper was announced one morning 'the arrival of the Dowager Viscountess Dalrymple, and her daughter, the Honourable Miss Carteret; and all the comfort of No. — Camden-place, was swept away for many days; for the Dalrymples ... were cousins of the Elliots; and the agony was, how to introduce themselves properly... Lady Dalrymple had taken a house ... in Laura-place and would be living in style.' (*Persuasion*, Penguin, 1986, p.161)

In Bath Anne renewed an old acquaintance, an old schoolfellow who had been very kind to her when she was unhappy and grieving for the loss of her mother. Mrs Smith had lodgings in Westgate Buildings. Anne visited her frequently and although her friend had changed very much she discovered rare and precious qualities. Reduced to great poverty, crippled by rheumatism:

> Yet, in spite of all this, Anne had reason to believe that she had moments only of languor and depression, to hours of occupation and enjoyment. How could it be? — She watched — observed — reflected — and finally determined that this was not a case of fortitude or of resignation only. — A submissive spirit might be patient, a strong understanding would supply resolution, but here was something more; here was that elasticity of mind, that disposition to be comforted, that power of turning readily from evil to good, and of finding employment which carried her out of herself, which was from Nature alone. It was the choicest gift of Heaven; and Anne viewed her friend as one of those instances in which, by a merciful appointment, it seems designed to counter-balance almost every other want. (*Ibid*. p.167)

This is indeed a most interesting passage. Anne Elliot attributes to her friend Mrs Smith this 'choicest gift of Heaven', but the fact that Anne recognized it for what it was and realized its value indicates that Anne herself possessed that rare gift — which in her difficult years had helped her 'to turn readily from evil to good'. And because we know that Jane Austen shared the same grief as Anne, remaining the same kind, warm-hearted woman, finding 'employment which carried her out of herself' — her novels are a brilliant example — we may attribute to her this 'choicest gift of Heaven'.

But there is still another interesting association to be mentioned. That 'elasticity of mind' so precious when unexpected and difficult circumstances are encountered seems to have been a quality of at least some members of the Austen family.

In her *Reminiscences* Caroline Austen was writing about her uncle Henry's bankruptcy and his decision to take holy orders, and to go to Oxford to obtain the necessary degree. 'He had very good abilities ... so ... no difficulties opposed his entrance into a profession to which he now turned with all the energy of a sanguine elastic nature.' And in 1819 Caroline, referring to her father's illness wrote that when he was reduced to indoor occupations he greatly enjoyed drawing and painting, adapting himself to this new situation with the help of Caroline's drawing-master.

It is interesting also what Anna Lefroy wrote about her uncle Henry Austen: 'He was like his father, blessed with a hopefulness of temper which adapting itself to all circumstances, even the most adverse, seemed to create a perpetual sunshine.' (William Austen-Leigh and Richard Arthur Austen-Leigh, *Jane Austen: Her Life and Letters — A family record*, p.49)

But writing these words 'choicest gift of Heaven' reminds me also of another heroine of another famous English novel, *Jane Eyre*. One day Mr Rochester, disguised as an old gypsy, analyses Jane's face and observes: 'that brow professes to say: "I can live alone ... I need not sell my soul to buy bliss. I have an inward treasure born with me, which can keep me alive if all extraneous delights should be withheld."' (Charlotte Brontë, *Jane Eyre*, Penguin, 1979, p.230)

That 'inward treasure' is the 'choicest gift of Heaven'. And it is moving and gratifying to see how these two great women writers agree on the most precious quality a human being can possess.

We find another autobiographical element in the description which Mrs Smith gives of her nurse Mrs Rooke: ' "She is a shrewd, intelligent, sensible woman ... she has a fund of good sense and observation which, as a companion, make her infinitely superior to thousands of those who ... received 'the best education in the world'."' (*Persuasion*, Penguin, 1986 p.168) Jane Austen was herself blessed with that 'fund of good sense and observation'.

In another circumstance we come to know — through Anne Elliot — a moving feature characteristic of Jane Austen herself. When trying to analyse Mr Elliot Anne was thinking:

> Mr Elliot was rational, discreet, polished — but he was not open. There was never a burst of feeling, any warmth of indignation or delight, at the evil or good of others. This, to Anne, was a decided imperfection... She prized the frank, the open-hearted, the eager character beyond all others... She felt that she could so much more depend upon the sincerity of those who sometimes looked or said a careless or a hasty thing, than of those whose presence of mind never varied, whose tongue never slipped. Mr Elliot was too generally agreeable. (*Ibid*. p.173)

With Anne Elliot we have frequented many streets and places in Bath. And then suddenly the name of one particular street makes us stop reading. It is a name well known to us because it has already been mentioned several times in another of Jane Austen's novels — in *Northanger Abbey* — and in connection with important events. It is Milsom Street in which General Tilney had taken lodgings with his son and daughter, Henry and Eleanor. In Milsom Street Catherine Morland is invited to dinner — and she is also invited to be the guest of the Tilney family in their home in Northanger Abbey. It is from Milsom Street that the journey to Northanger Abbey starts, after a large breakfast has been taken together. And here, in *Persuasion*, this street is again mentioned and an important event takes place in Milsom Street. For it is in Milsom Street that Anne Elliot meets Frederick Wentworth for the first time after he has regained his freedom, after Louisa Musgrove's engagement to Captain Benwick. The encounter takes place at Molland's: Molland's bakery and confectionery shop. Frederick is taken by surprise and seems to be more confused to see her than she has ever noticed previously. It is a short meeting but rich in consequence. Is there any doubt that in real life Milsom Street has been associated with important moments in the relationship between Jane Austen and Tom Lefroy? Maybe we shall never come to know when and in what circumstances they walked along this busy shopping street: they probably went into Molland's shop. But we may assume that they were happy circumstances whose memory Jane was glad to revive in mentioning the name of Milsom Street again.[1]

The whole party was to meet one evening at a concert in the octagon room — Sir Walter Elliot, his two daughters, Mrs Clay, Mr Elliot, Captain Wentworth, Lady Russell, Lady Dalrymple, her daughter. During a conversation with Frederick Wentworth Anne says that she likes Lyme and she explains why this small seaside resort has so much charm for her in spite of the distress caused by Louisa's accident there. Anne's words have a personal touch and could have been said by Jane herself: ' "I have travelled so little, that every fresh place would be interesting to me — but there is real beauty at Lyme." ' The conversation with Frederick takes a very personal turn and Anne while listening to him:

> was struck, gratified, confused and beginning to breathe very quick, and feel hundred things in a moment... Her happiness was from within... She was thinking only of the last half hour ... His choice of subjects, his expressions, and still more his manner and look, had been such as she could see in only one light ... all, all declared that he had a heart returning to her at least ... She could not contemplate the change as implying less. — He must love her. (*Ibid.* pp.194–5)

It is a moving passage. And if there still remains a doubt about the true identity of Frederick Wentworth, this doubt is definitely dissipated two pages later: Lady Dalrymple, watching Captain Wentworth is sensitive to his charm and exclaims: ' "A very fine young man indeed! More air than one often sees in Bath.

— Irish, I dare say." ' (*Ibid.* p.197)

We know that Tom Lefroy was Irish: that Jane in a letter to her sister Cassandra refers to 'my Irish friend'. The long passage above is but a dream of happiness in which Jane indulged twenty years later in Chawton — alone — in front of her small sheets of paper. We can be sure that it was sweet to write down these words: ' "A very fine young man indeed! More air than one often sees in Bath. — Irish, I dare say." '

Let us also remember that 'Irish' was always to be for Jane synonymous with ease and charm — in her letters, in her novels. In a letter to Cassandra from Lyme (Letter 39, dated 14 September 1804) she writes about a man who asked her to dance with him: 'I think he must be Irish by his ease.'

Years later, writing in *Emma* about Miss Campbell's fiancé Mr Dixon, who was Irish, she says: ' "He is a most amiable, charming young man." ' We also learn that he was pressing his friends to come to Dublin and promising to take them to his country seat — a beautiful place.

'It was very natural, you know, that he should like to speak of his own place while he was paying his addresses — and as Jane used to be very often walking out with them ... heard everything he might be telling Miss Campbell about his own home in Ireland... he had shewn them some drawings of the place, views that he had taken himself... Jane was quite longing to go to Ireland, from his account of things.' (*Emma*, Penguin, 1986, p.173)

Like a piece of mother-of-pearl inlaid in the neutral course of the novel, these passages evoke young Jane Austen listening to Tom Lefroy's enthusiastic descriptions of Ireland, admiring his sketches, longing to see Ireland: ' *"Jane was quite longing to go to Ireland."* ' (Author's italics)

In chapter 22 we read that Mrs Musgrove has arrived in Bath with her two daughters and had taken lodgings at the White Hart. Anne is happy to hear that Louisa and Henrietta will soon marry. She values the kindness and wisdom of Mr and Mrs Musgrove who ' "do everything to confer happiness [on their children]. What a blessing to young people to be in such hands! Your father and mother seem so totally free from all those ambitious feelings which have led to so much misconduct and misery, both in young and old!" ' (*Persuasion*, Penguin, 1986, p.223)

It is clear that in the novel Anne Elliot makes an allusion to Lady Russell's ambitious feelings on her behalf, persuading her to break her engagement with Frederick Wentworth because she thinks him not worthy of Anne. But in writing these lines Jane Austen must have had in mind the ambition that inspired Mrs Lefroy — twenty years earlier — to persuade and send young Tom Lefroy away in order to prevent him from marrying her. Their separation brought grief to her and, as she writes in her novel, 'misery to young and old' — meaning, no doubt, her father who loved her dearly and must have suffered as much as his daughter. Fiction and reality meet.

THE UPPER LAKE OF KILLARNEY, IRELAND
Reproduced from G. N. Wright: *Ireland Illustrated*, London 1831, by courtesy of Trinity College Library, Dublin.

THE UPPER LAKE OF KILLARNEY, IRELAND
Reproduced from G. N. Wright: *Ireland Illustrated*, London 1831, by courtesy of Trinity College Library, Dublin.

'...he had shewn them some drawings of the place, views that he had taken himself. He is a most amiable, charming young man, I believe. *Jane was quite longing to go to Ireland,* from his account of things.'
(Jane Austen, *Emma*) (Author's italics)

One day at the White Hart a large company was gathered to attend Mrs Musgrove and her daughters. Captain Harville, a friend of Captain Wentworth, was also present. A lively discussion started between him and Anne. Hearing him praise his dead sister's love and fidelity for Captain Benwick Anne replies that it would be the nature of any woman who truly loved. To his rather sceptical smile Anne answers with warmth:

> 'We certainly do not forget you, so soon as you forget us. It is, perhaps, our fate rather than our merit. We cannot help ourselves. We live at home, quiet, confined, and our feelings prey upon us. You are forced on exertion. You have always a profession, pursuits, business of some sort or other, to take you back into the world immediately, and continual occupation and change soon weaken impressions... All the privilege I claim for my own sex (it is not a very enviable one, you need not covet it) is that of loving longest, when existence or when hope is gone.' (*Persuasion*, Penguin, 1986, pp.236–8)

In the novel, Captain Wentworth is in the same room, but at some distance away and occupied in writing a letter. He is not supposed to be able to hear what is said during the conversation — but he hears it all. Anne's passionate words in defence of woman's constancy in love convince him that she still loves him. What follows is known and the happy ending belongs only to fiction.

In her last novel Jane Austen has shown the world that her sparkling wit and playful mind were but one facet of her personality. In *Persuasion* Jane Austen opened the doors to her innermost soul and we discover a sensitive and vulnerable woman capable of long-lasting, tender and passionate love.

Her strong feelings, presented with great restraint, have long been underestimated. Because the identification of Anne Elliot with Jane Austen has often been contradicted with various arguments let us pause for a moment to consider this topic. We meet the idea that emotions expressed in *Persuasion* belong also to the woman who wrote the novel in an interesting article by Robert T. K. Wallace, *Jane Austen's Neglected Song Book* (The Jane Austen Society, Report of the Year 1979).

It seems that in the 1778 Song Book which Jane received from her elders, she continued to add to it herself and of the twenty un-numbered manuscript songs, at least eighteen are love-songs, and a majority of those songs are about lovers who are separated.

> To a curious degree, most of these songs anticipate either the situation or the mood of Anne Elliot in *Persuasion*... The words and the notes are consistently poignant. The most interesting songs, perhaps, are the 'hidden' ones — the ones whose existence is not even acknowledged in the table of contents. (Robert K. Wallace, *Jane Austen's Neglected Song Book*, Annual Report, 1979, pp.121–5).

The first song, 'Susan', is addressed to a woman who is separated from a sailor whom she loves. It begins:

Oh Susan, Susan lovely dear,
My vows shall ever true remain
Let me kiss off this falling tear
We only part to meet again.

The second song is also about parted lovers:

Why tarries my Love?
Ah where does he rove?
My love is long absent from me.

The third 'hidden' song is from Sheridan's *The Stranger*, and the music is marked 'Plaintive':

I have a silent sorrow here,
A Grief I'll ne'er impart;
It breathes no Sigh, it sheds no tear,
But it consumes my heart.

Song number 8, which precedes 'Susan' and the other 'hidden' songs, is very impressive. It is written in a manuscript hand, almost certainly by Jane Austen. It begins with the words:

How imperfect is expression
Some emotions to impart

And ends with the words:

what faultring dying
Language would but cannot tell.

The author of the article gives a hint as to the possible relationship that the songs about parted lovers may have had to the life or fiction of the woman who wrote *Persuasion*. So we may conclude that the emotions which Jane did not put into words throughout her life until she wrote *Persuasion*, she expressed in the words and the music of the songs in this most intriguing '1778' Song Book.

Most interesting for us at this point is that Jane Austen's last novel *Persuasion* has been associated with Mozart's last piano concerto in B flat, K.595, composed in January 1791 a few months before his death. (Robert K. Wallace, *Jane Austen and Mozart — classical Equilibrium in Fiction and Music*). In his great biography of Mozart, Alfred Einstein is writing about this last piano concerto: 'God has allowed Mozart to express his suffering.' The parallel is striking indeed, as we may paraphrase Einstein and write: 'God has allowed Jane Austen to express her suffering in her last novel.'

After this digression let us return to the novel — to the last pages of *Persuasion* and their message.

We may consider Anne Elliot's words in defence of woman's constancy in love to have been Jane Austen's own testament as a message to reach — from a remote past, over the years, over land and sea — her Irish friend. She knew, and in her last hours it must have been a sweet thought, that one day Thomas Lefroy would read Anne Elliot's story — and while reading would remember with tenderness Jane Austen, their encounters in Bath, the balls in Basingstoke, their contract of mutual agreeableness for one evening.

Reader, perhaps you have been thinking that the author of this work has been swept away on the wings of romantic fantasy, indulging herself in dreams of everlasting love. And if this is indeed the way you are thinking here is a last attempt to convince you. In a letter to her niece Fanny Knight (Letter 103, dated 8 November 1814) Jane Austen is writing about a young man with very special qualities of heart and mind: 'There are such beings in the World perhaps, one in a Thousand... Where Grace and Spirit are united to Worth, where Manners are equal to the Heart and Understanding, but such a person may not come in your way...'

In her youth Jane had met such a young man. Is it surprising that she could never forget him? In another letter (Letter 106, dated 30 November 1814) addressed to this same niece, Jane warns her: 'nothing can be compared to the misery of being bound *without* Love, bound to one and preferring another...'

We can now perhaps better understand what happened at Manydown; during the night that followed Harry Bigg Wither's proposal Jane must have had that insight. On the following morning she acted in consequence and broke off the engagement.

The day after I completed this chapter I finished reading R. W. Chapman's book *Jane Austen's Letters to her sister Cassandra and others*. While I was reading the last pages, Cassandra's account of Jane's last days and last hours I felt that I was parting from a dear friend. I had shared Jane's life through the five hundred pages of the book and it was as if I had really been there in the small Winchester room, in Winchester cathedral, grieving. And then, slowly turning the page, I came across the coat-of-arms of the Austen family and I read the motto: *Qui invidit minor est* (who envies is petty-minded). Wonderful words, appeasing words. They helped me to understand even better the Austen spirit — transmitted from generation to generation, attaining its full bloom in our Jane Austen, in her generous impulses, her large-hearted charity, her power of intuitive sympathy. And I closed the book with a smile of gratitude.

COAT-OF-ARMS OF THE AUSTEN FAMILY

The motto: 'Qui invidit minor est' — Who envies is small-minded.

Reproduced from R. W. Chapman: *Jane Austen's Letters to her sister Cassandra and others*, Oxford University Press, 1952

1. In part one, I refer to evidence that in November 1797 Mrs Austen and her two daughters were in Bath at the same time as the Lefroy family. Those were the happy days that Jane and Tom Lefroy spent together in Bath. We still do not know if they were the only ones.

III SOMEBODY JANE AUSTEN WILL NEVER FORGET OR FORGIVE

'The French call me: "*fou d'aristocratie*" — they care nothing for ancestors. Is it nothing to be descendant of geniuses, statesmen, legislators, heroes? ... The greatest man in European history is Charlemagne and from him my blood flows through three hundred channels.' — Sir Egerton Brydges *The Autobiography*

There is somebody — though by no means a member of the Austen family — whose name is mentioned in everything of importance that has ever been written about Jane Austen, beginning with *A Memoir* by J. E. Austen-Leigh, written in 1869 and continuing up to the last important biography, *Jane Austen: Her Life* by Park Honan in 1987, not to mention the books by David Cecil or R. W. Chapman.

It is Sir Egerton Brydges, an apparently insignificant character whose name appears here and there as that of a supernumerary person who occasionally crossed Jane Austen's path as the younger brother of Mrs Lefroy from Ashe — a neighbour of the Austen family. He was first mentioned in *A Memoir* because he had known Jane as a young girl and had written a few words about her in *The Autobiography*. It seems that this was the main reason why he was ever mentioned. Knowing the decisive role that Mrs Lefroy had played in Jane Austen's life — her interference in Jane's relationship with Tom Lefroy — I thought that it might be interesting for me to get better acquainted with Sir Egerton Brydges, Mrs Lefroy's brother.

In writing about the drama that for some years had opposed Steventon to Ashe it has been more or less taken for granted by Jane Austen's biographers that it was Mrs Lefroy who was responsible for the abrupt ending of the romance between her nephew and their young neighbour Jane Austen.

In all the biographies we read that it was Mrs Lefroy who in alarm had 'hurried away' Tom Lefroy to prevent more mischief. Nobody ever seemed to have suspected that Mrs Lefroy's brother might have had some part in what happened.

My attention was first awakened by a coincidence: in *A Memoir* J. E. Austen-Leigh, after reproducing a passage from Sir Egerton Brydges's *The*

Autobiography describing young Jane, adds: 'one may wish that Sir Egerton had dwelt rather longer on the subject of these memoirs instead of being drawn away by his extreme love for genealogies to her great-grandmother and ancestors.' (A *Memoir*, 1869, Penguin, 1986, p.306)

I immediately connected these very words — 'his extreme love for genealogies' — with a rather unpleasant minor character in Jane Austen's last novel, *Persuasion*. This is Sir Walter Elliot, who also had an extreme love for genealogy. Here is a passage from the novel in which he is described:

'Sir Walter Elliot, of Kellynch Hall in Somersetshire was a man who, for his own amusement, never took up any book but the Baronetage; ... and there ... he could read his own history with an interest which never failed — this was the page at which the favourite volume always opened: "ELLIOT OF KELLYNCH HALL".' (*Persuasion*, Penguin, 1986, p.35)

If Jane did attribute to one of her unpleasant characters this love of genealogy which she had met in real life in Sir Egerton Brydges, no doubt she must have had a reason for resenting him. And what could the reason be? Being Mrs Lefroy's brother, he must have helped her to persuade and convince young Tom Lefroy that it was foolish to marry a poor girl. He must have used his manly prestige, his own experience, and succeeded where a woman might have failed. From *The Autobiography* we know that he was very attached to his elder sister whom he also very much admired.

The Autobiography of Sir Egerton Brydges does indeed confirm the analogy between him and some of Jane Austen's unpleasant characters. Let us run over the history of his life.

He was born on 30 November 1762 at Wootton Court in Kent. He grew up in surroundings where family history and family ancestors were very important and often talked of with veneration. Very early on he showed a liking for poetry. He had an elder sister to whom he was strongly attached. As a young man he made vain efforts for many years to get into Parliament. An elder brother of his had claims on the title of Baron of Chandos.

In 1792 he bought an old manor in Denton, where he lived until October 1810. He married at twenty-two 'much too early — without an income adequate to my habits, unless with great economy'. (Egerton Brydges, *The Autobiography*, 1834, p.15)

Sir Egerton's wife was Elizabeth Byrche, niece of Thomas Barrett of Lee Priory. In 1810 Sir Egerton moved to Lee Priory which his eldest son Thomas Barrett Brydges had inherited on the death — in 1803 — of his mother's uncle, Thomas Barrett. Lee Priory was a Jacobean house remodelled in the Gothic taste by James Wyatt for Thomas Barrett between 1782 and 1790. In his article 'Jane Austen and Egerton Brydges' (The Jane Austen Society, Report for the Year 1976) David Gilson suggests that Jane Austen might have seen Lee Priory, through her connection with Sir Egerton, when she visited Kent, adding: 'It is tempting to consider the house as at least a partial prototype of Northanger Abbey.' (Brydges' son inherited Lee Priory in the year when the first version of that novel was finished and sold to Crosby.) This might reinforce my statement that General Tilney, the proud owner of Northanger Abbey was inspired by Sir Egerton Brydges.

Sir Egerton's life was one of waste and disorder — 'I knew not what my income was ... kept imperfect accounts and everyone cheated me ... I worked by fits...' (*Ibid.* p.21) How very like Sir Walter Elliot, one might exclaim!

Also, like Sir Walter Elliot, Sir Egerton was very handsome. Park Honan describes him as 'large-eyed and delicate, with a brown lock drooping over a tragically noble forehead'. This description evokes a would-be Byronic personality. We can easily imagine Sir Egerton strolling around the Villa Diodati on the shores of Lake Geneva, dreaming of the great romantic poet. With a smile we may also wonder: was his house adorned with an incredible number of mirrors as was Kellynch Hall?

He goes on to say: 'I had a good collection of biographical, genealogical and historical works ... and I was well conversant with their content. I combined, compared and criticized.' (*Ibid.* p.22)

He had a large family of children. His two elder sisters were married in Hampshire. Although he enjoyed staying with his sisters in Hampshire, and was happiest of all with Anne, Mrs Lefroy from Ashe, where he used to spend long periods, he did not enjoy country society: 'I never could bear the talk of country squires.' (*Ibid.* p.85)

He must have been a rather unbalanced person and he often felt persecuted: 'I saw mean men, every day perching over my head and insulting me, conspiring to calumniate and injure me... The claim to the barony of Chandos was poison to our neighbours...' (*Ibid.* p.29)

He must have had a suspicious mind and was neither easy nor conciliatory. He recognized that he was a bad visitor — he did not return calls. He took his refuge in books: 'I had ardour for books, but read without method... I lived on literature, but in eagerness of fever and ended in ennui...' (*Ibid.* p.29)

In 1779 he visited Cambridge and Winchester. He found local jealousies and enmities. Disgusted, he returned to his books: 'My pursuit of literature was pure, blind, unregulated love of literature...' (*Ibid.* p.70)

In Denton he had much leisure 'but my mind was distracted and therefore could pursue nothing which had no excitement ... I could do nothing which required a regular perseverance of labour ... whatever I did was fitful and transitory and required the stimulus of variety.' (*Ibid.* pp.78–9)

At forty-two he still had hopes of a literary or a political career. There was one topic of conversation which never tired him: the genealogies of all his acquaintances. Since early childhood — at eight or nine years of age — he had contracted a passion for biography, reading *Biographia Britannica*. 'I had the book constantly in my hands.' (*Ibid.* p.99)

He had a pessimistic view of life:

VILLA DIODATI, COLOGNY, LAKE OF GENEVA (Yohann Poppel)

Reproduced by courtesy of the Centre d'iconographie genevoise, Geneva.

> Who are the people that make a future: the crafty and the selfish. All the affairs of the world are managed by artifice and intrigue. These are carried into literature, which never succeeds without rude contrivance and adroitness of addresses. A publisher cannot get off a book by the mere force of its merits. (*Ibid.* p.103)

As already stated, Sir Egerton Brydges had been brought up from early childhood in the knowledge of his great ancestors: 'I heard from early infancy of the rise and grandeur of my ancestor Lord Chancellor Egerton, and the grandeur of my royal blood.' (*Ibid.* p.105)

Writing about the genealogy of Dr W. Egerton (died 26 February 1737) that goes back to Princess Mary Tudor, youngest daughter of King Henry VII and widow of Louis XII, King of France, he emphasizes: 'This was the highest blood in the kingdom.' (*Ibid.* p.152) He was always observant of heraldic symbols!

When he was not busy with genealogy he wrote poems. But: 'I wrote no long poems. I undertook no great work; I finished very few things.' (*Ibid.* p.129)

> Poetry was taught to me by my eldest sister Anne, born in March 1748, married to the Rev. George Lefroy, the rector of Compton, later also of Ashe. He was the youngest son of Anthony Lefroy, who had an elder son Anthony, who retiring from the army settled in Limerick in Ireland, and was father of Thomas, now (1834) MP for the University of Dublin. (*Ibid.* p.136)

This is the only mention so far of Thomas Lefroy, his sister's nephew, in *The Autobiography*, because of his wish to avoid writing about persons who were still living.

That Sir Egerton Brydges was very attached to his sister Anne Lefroy will be evident from the following passage:

> My eldest sister Anne, born March 1748, married to the Rev. George Lefroy, the rector of Compton in Surrey, was one of the most amiable and eloquent women I ever knew, and was universally beloved and admired. She was a great reader, and her rapidity of apprehension was lightning. She wrote elegant and flourishing verses on occasional subjects with great ease. She was fond of society, and was the life of every party, into which she entered. She died by a fall from a horse in December 1804... In her hospitable house I spent many of the happiest days of my life. (*Ibid.* pp.136–7)

Attached as Sir Egerton was to his sister one can easily understand that he took an interest in everything that was important to her, trying to be helpful and giving her advice.

During 1796–8[1] the Lefroy family was to witness the increasing affection between Tom Lefroy and Jane Austen. Since they believed her to be an heiress, the romance was at first observed with pleasure. But when it was known that after all the girl had nothing (this was the 'disappointment' referred to in later years, in the Lefroy family) the Lefroy family did everything it could to put an end to the relationship. The role of Sir Egerton Brydges must have been important indeed in convincing young Tom Lefroy, using his manly and aristocratic prestige — and for the sensitive young man the powerful argument was that he must not disappoint his generous benefactor, his wealthy uncle Langlois! The end of the story is known.

There is still something to be said about one of the principal actors of this drama of long ago, namely Mrs Anne Lefroy. In Caroline Austen's *Reminiscences* a small, apparently anodyne incident is mentioned — tragic because it happened on the very day of Mrs Lefroy's death, interesting because it throws light on her character. Here is the passage:

> 1804, December 16th. 'Died Mrs Lefroy of Ashe'. On the 21st my father buried her. She was greatly lamented and her end was a sad one. She was riding a very quiet horse, attended by a servant, as usual. My father saw her in Overton, and she observed the animal she rode was *so stupid and lazy*, she could scarcely make him canter. My father rode homeward, she staying to do some errands in Overton; next morning the news of her death reached Steventon. After getting to the top of Overton Hill, the horse seemed to be running away — it was not known whether anything had frightened him — the servant, unwisely, rode up to catch the bridle rein — missed his hold and the animal darted off faster. He could not give any clear account, but it was supposed that Mrs Lefroy in her terror, threw herself off, and fell heavily on the hard ground. She never spoke afterwards, and she died in a few hours. She was a woman most highly gifted, and had the power of attaching and influencing all who came near her in an unusual manner. (Caroline Austen, *Reminiscences*, 1874 The Jane Austen Society, 1986, p.8)

For anybody who loves animals and especially horses there is no need to add any comment. But your name, Madam Lefroy, will be saved from oblivion thanks to your young neighbour Jane Austen, who much trusted and admired you and whom you thought unworthy to marry your nephew.

Meanwhile the claim of the Chandos barony continues. More and more Sir Egerton becomes familiar with the history of the Brydges:

> The peerage was created by patent at the coronation of Philip and Mary in 1554, but was only a confirmation of one of the Anglo-Norman peerages which had come by marriage into the Brydges family in the reign of Edward III... (*The Autobiography*, 1834, p.217)

ENTRANCE FRONT OF ASPLEY HOUSE, BEDFORDSHIRE

Not unlike the Rectory of Ashe — home of Reverend George and Mrs Anne Lefroy.

Reproduced from: *Bath and Bristol with the Counties of Somerset and Gloucester*, London 1829, by courtesy of the Rijksmuseum Stichting, Amsterdam.

...They are, as far as I can trace, now all extinct ... And here I stand alone — all but my own son; and my brother and his only son, a cornet in the Third Dragoon Guards. (*Ibid.* p.218)

How familiar Sir Egerton was with the pedigree of the gentry of the Cheshire county, from which a great portion of his own blood was derived, is seen in the following passage:

> The earls palatine of Chester had their court of barons, of whom a list is given by Dugdale, under that earldom. The Egertons and Cholmondeleys are sprung from the same male stock, who were barons of Malpas. The Tattons are supposed, with reason, to be a younger branch of another of these barons — The Masseys, who possessed anciently the lordship of Tatton; but which, in later times, was the property of Lord Chancellor Egerton, and thence came to my great-grandfather Thomas Egerton, who died 1685, younger son of John, second earl of Bridgewater. His grandson, Samuel Egerton, MP for Cheshire, having lost his only daughter a few months before his death, devised it, after his sister's death, to her son William Tatton of Withenshaw, who took the name of Egerton, and was father of the present Wilbraham Egerton, Esq. of Tatton, late MP for Cheshire.
> One of these barons of the earls palatine of this county was of the ancient family of Mainwaring of Pever. About their early quality a memorable contest happened in the reign of Charles II between the head of this house and Sir Peter Leicester, the Cheshire historian. It appeared by an authentic document, that he stood so high that he had married a co-heir of the last of these earls palatine, Hugh Kevelive, Earl of Chester, and accordingly always quartered his arms. Sir Peter Leicester, probably from provincial jealousy, took it into his head to contend that this co-heir must have been illegitimate. A war of pamphlets took place between the two baronets, all of which are now very scarce and very curious. It ended in a trial at law on a feigned issue, and a verdict was given in favour of the legitimacy of this ancestress of Sir Thomas Mainwaring, on the ground of a deed of frank-marriage by the earl to this daughter, as a dowry to Mainwaring, because it was held to be law that gifts in frank-marriage could only take place where the daughter was legitimate.
> Sir Henry Mainwaring of Pever, the last baronet of the elder branch, died unmarried 1797. He left his ancient estates and the name to the heir of his mother, who re-married a Whetenhall by whom she had Thomas Whetenhall, or Wittenhall, who took the name of Mainwaring, and was father of Henry, created a baronet 12th May, 1804, and married Sophia, sister of Lord Combermere, by whom he has a son, Harry, who married in February, 1732, Emma, eldest daughter of the late William Tatton, Esq. of Wittenshaw.
> Neither I nor Mr Lodge can trace any descendants now remaining from

Sir Randle Mainwaring, elder brother of Edmund Mainwaring, and uncle of Sir William Mainwaring; so that it seems I am a co-representative of this most ancient and honourable family with Mr Egerton of Tatton, who is descended from my grandfather Egerton's elder brother. See 'Stemmata Illustrie', Paris, 1826, fol. p.12. (*Ibid.* pp.353–5)

His passion for genealogy, his worship of aristocracy, is best expressed in his own words: 'It is natural for me to have fondness for the old aristocracy of England ... the old nobility were a body useful to the people and beloved by them.' (*Ibid.* p.347) And also: 'The French call me: *"fou d'aristocratie"* — they care nothing for ancestors. Is it nothing to be the descendant of geniuses, statesmen, legislators, heroes? ... The greatest man in European history is Charlemagne and from him my blood flows through three hundred channels.' (Egerton Brydges: *The Autobiography*, Vol.II pp.137–8)

In 1800 his older brother died and he inherited the peerage and the estate. It is worth mentioning that between 1789 and 1800 Sir Egerton Brydges was in the army, accepting a troop in a regiment of Funcible Cavalry. We may ask ourselves: 'Was it a coincidence that it was a General (General Tilney) who interfered and tried to make an end to the romance between Catherine Morland and Henry Tilney in *Northanger Abbey?*'

In Volume I of *The Autobiography* Sir Egerton Brydges was mainly concerned with the history and genealogy of his family. In Volume II his interest turns to literature, poetry, novels, writers and poets. It was in this context that he wrote the famous passage about Jane Austen, who, at that time (1834), was already a well-known novelist. Here is the passage for which Sir Egerton Brydges will be for ever connected with her — Jane Austen was interesting for him as a writer but also because of the aristocratic background of her mother:

> The nearest neighbours of the Lefroys were the Austens of Steventon. I remember Jane Austen, the novelist, as a child. She was intimate with Mrs Lefroy, and much encouraged by her. Her mother was a Miss Leigh, whose paternal grandmother was sister to the first Duke of Chandos. Mr Austen was of Kentish family, of which several branches have been settled in the Weald of Kent... When I knew Jane Austen, I never suspected that she was an authoress; but my eyes told me that she was fair and handsome, slight and elegant, but with cheeks a little too full. (quoted in J. E. Austen-Leigh, *A Memoir*, Penguin, 1986 p.306)

As in his *Imaginative Biography*, Sir Egerton Brydges mentions in Volume II of *The Autobiography* the names of many famous and less famous writers, commenting on their work. Among them are: Johnson, Boswell, Bacon, Raleigh, Clarendon, Chatham, Byron, Sir Nathaniel Wraxhall, Robert Peel, Gray, Cowper, Milton, Barrett, Pearson, the Duke of Roxburghe.

Very early we come to know his dislike of novels, of fiction in general. 'I hate those fictions which represent society in its worst and meanest artificialities — those petty passions of accidental and temporary life and manners, those odious fashions of folly and vanity.' (Egerton Brydges, *Imaginative Biography*, 1834, p.140) And also: 'Love of books tells the sudden decay of any spirit.' (*Ibid.* p.195) He names Fielding, Richardson, Miss Burney, commenting: 'they have long ceased to interest... What tiresome and nonsensical things are the old French romances of Louis XIV's days.' (*Ibid.* p.197)

A little further we read:

> He who in common language is called a wit, has nothing to do but to tell the brilliancies of conversation, the collisions of rival observers, and the comic effect of the marked manners of those who spend their existence upon the public stage in conflicting groups; but this is to encourage all the passions which wisdom and virtue ought to do their utmost to control and eradicate. (*Ibid.* p.240)

Among all these bitter comments it is refreshing to read a passage which Sir Egerton quotes from a letter by Southey in which he mentions Jane Austen. Here is the passage:

> Her novels are more true to nature, and have (for my sympathies) passages of finer feelings than any other of this age. She was a person of whom I have heard so well, and think so highly, that I regret not having seen her, nor ever having had an opportunity of testifying to her the respect which I felt for her. (Robert Southey, 8 April 1830)

If Sir Egerton Brydges's love for genealogy often reminds us of Sir Walter Elliot, in the second volume of his autobiography the many sarcastic comments on literature and novel writers remind us of another rather unpleasant character of Jane Austen's novels: young John Thorpe from *Northanger Abbey*. Silly, snobbish and superficial he dislikes books and is never ashamed to say so. When Catherine Morland ventures to ask a question which has long been in her thoughts: ' "Have you ever read 'Udolpho', Mr Thorpe?" ' he exclaims: ' " 'Udolpho'! Oh, Lord! not I; I never read novels. I have something else to do... Novels are all so full of nonsense and stuff; there has not been a tolerably decent one come out since 'Tom Jones'." ' (Jane Austen, *Northanger Abbey*, Penguin, 1987 p.69)
And about Camilla he says: 'Such unnatural stuff... it is the horridest nonsense you can imagine...'

It is interesting and amusing to contrast with Sir Egerton Brydges's and young John Thorpe's pejorative comments on novels, a passage in which Henry Tilney expresses his opinion (which is also Jane Austen's own opinion) on people who dislike reading novels: ' "The person, be it gentleman or lady, who has no pleasure in a good novel, must be intolerably stupid." ' (*Ibid.* p.121)

It is easy to guess that at the time when she wrote her first novel (*Northanger Abbey*) Jane must have known the shortcomings of the man who had influenced her life, Sir Egerton Brydges.

This knowledge is also confirmed by a passage in a letter to her sister Cassandra, (Letter 12, dated Saturday 25 November 1798). Writing about Sir Egerton's book *Fitz-Albini* she expresses her opinion on it: 'I am not disappointed by Egerton's book for I expected nothing better. Never did any book carry more internal evidence of its author. Every sentiment is completely Egerton...'

The verdict is lashing: Jane Austen will never forget Sir Egerton Brydges. He will live for ever in her novels: in General Tilney — moody, arrogant, pusillanimous and a lover of show; in young John Thorpe vain, boasting, self-sufficient; in Sir Edgar Elliot: a limited person, obsessed by genealogy, a bad manager of his fortune, recklessly spendthrift, avid of titles and rank, a puppet of circumstances. And in her last attempt to write — *Sanditon*, the novel she could not finish — a few months before her death, Sir Egerton was still haunting her memory as a model for Sir Edward Denham — the silly, womanizing aristocrat, with his pompous comments on romantic poetry and romantic poets — perorating 'of the *indescribable* emotions they excite in the mind of sensibility'. (Jane Austen, *Sanditon*, Penguin, 1974 p.184)

So far I have tried to analyse the relationship that existed between Jane Austen and Sir Egerton Brydges. Nearly two hundred years have passed since he interfered with her life and justice has been done. Sir Egerton Brydges's name will be remembered only thanks to the young girl whom he once thought too poor and too obscure to marry his sister's nephew, Tom Lefroy, and who was to become one of England's greatest women writers.

I propose to end this chapter gently. At the age of seventy-two, in a foreign country, Sir Egerton has changed. Life and time have made him more human and more humble. He writes about his anxiety to take farewell, looks back, sums up his life. I will end this chapter with his own words:

> I feel anxiety to take farewell. I have written with sincerity... I have passed the last 16 years on the Continent... I have given way to melancholy... Old age has not hardened my heart ... has mellowed my intellect... I have enlarged my candour and benevolence... I have conquered the passions of envy and jealousy and have learned to despise wealth, show and luxury... I have borne deprivations with fortitude and cease to wish for anything beyond a competence... I have not lost my calmness or cheerfulness beneath frightful and almost incredible injustice and wrong... I am more delighted with the grandeur and beauty of nature than ever in the glow and

enthusiasm of youth... I love good poetry as much... I have not been a nursling of fortune. My life has been a life of difficulties, dangers, misfortunes, oppressions, wrongs, spoliations and defeats... I have miscalculated my means, and thrown away my strength... Family intrigues of my own generation have added to these bars on the way of my success in life... If I might have gone more afield early in life I might have escaped this... I was too unwise ... I had a fondness for the spots of my nativity and their vicinage... I believe that I am mild, well-wishing, still warm and energetic, with a glowing imagination and a trembling heart ... ready to be pleased, melting to kindness; visionary as a child, yet not unskilled in life; more ductile than becomes my years, more solitary than consistent with wordly vision.

'What a fanciful picture he has drawn of himself!' my traducers will exclaim... Oh! surly, stern, misanthropic, captious, contradictory, furious, confused, moody, melancholy, querulous, arrogant, vain, awkward, dull, pusillanimous, a lover of show, recklessly expensive, avid of titles and rank and aspiring to all employments without any regard to his fitness for them... Some day these calumnies will be forgotten...

Geneva May 1834

(Egerton Brydges: *The Autobiography*, Vols. I and II, 1834 pp.413–30).

Note

1. The date 1798 is based on the following:
During a visit Mrs Lefroy paid to the Austen family in Steventon in November 1798, she did not mention Tom Lefroy although she knew how important it was for Jane to hear from him. Commenting on this visit, Jane wrote to Cassandra: 'Of her nephew she did not once mention the name to me, and I was too proud to make any enquiries; but on my father's afterwards asking where he was, I learnt that he was gone back to London in his way to Ireland, where he is called to the Bar and means to practise.' (Letter 11, dated Saturday, 17 November, 1798) One conclusion offers itself: only someone who has recently been offended is too proud to make enquiries about a person involved in the offence. So we may conclude that the abrupt departure of Tom Lefroy must have taken place quite recently — which means that their relationship lasted till 1798. My suspicion is confirmed by the following passage in David Cecil's book *A Portrait of Jane Austen*: 'In fact the flirtation was not over [after quoting from a letter Jane wrote in 1796: "At length the day has come in which I am to flirt my last with Mr Tom Lefroy..."]: it lingered on into 1798 and it seems as if Jane's feelings became a little more serious. Certainly Tom Lefroy's feelings for her did; and openly enough to worry his uncle and aunt, who thought him too young and too poor to think of marriage. To stop this, they immediately packed him off home to Ireland.' (David Cecil, *A Portrait of Jane Austen*, Penguin, 1986, p.76)

IV AND WHAT ABOUT THE ABSENT HERO, TOM LEFROY?

'A dutiful boy with such a kind disposition and affectionate heart.'
Dr Burrowes, Trinity College, Dublin

Yet the story was not ended. I have been wondering for a long time about the evident contradiction between the image which Jane Austen has left of Tom Lefroy in *Northanger Abbey* and in *Persuasion*, her first and her last novels, and the description that some members of the Lefroy family, and influenced by them, the biographers of Jane Austen, presented of him.

Was Tom Lefroy the fine, affectionate, brilliant young man with a strong Christian faith and high moral principles like Henry Tilney and Captain Wentworth, or was he 'the dashing young Irishman whose brief visit to his uncle in Hampshire brought Jane an exciting partner and a refreshing new face in the predictable line-up of local bachelors at balls and dances?' (Helen Lefroy, *Strangers* Report Jane Austen Society, 1982). Was he the brilliant young man, courting, flirting and then leaving broken hearts behind him, carelessly starting his juridical career in Ireland and marrying a well provided for and well connected girl?

Jane Austen's biographers have told us who Tom Lefroy was, have described his family history, evoking the wealthy French Huguenot ancestors who came to England in the sixteenth century. Mention is made of his grandfather Anthony Lefroy who joined the banking house of Peter Langlois and married his daughter Elizabeth. They had three children: Anthony Peter (Tom's father), George, who was to marry Anne Brydges, and Phoebe. Anthony Peter made what was then considered an 'imprudent alliance at an early age ... only 23 years of age, and a very junior officer had, when quartered in Limerick, fallen in love with Ann Gardner, daughter of a local squire of modest means. In 1765 Ensign Anthony Peter and Ann Gardner were married secretly by a regimental chaplain...' The marriage was kept secret in order not to antagonize the wealthy Langlois uncles. Five girls were born — and the secret was still kept. When the first boy was born in 1776 — our Tom Lefroy — the moment had come to legitimize the union and an official marriage took place in Limerick cathedral. Four more boys were to follow.

As at the time there were no male descendants in the Langlois family, Elizabeth's (née Langlois) children, as the only Langlois descendants, were surrounded with much love and care. When Anthony Peter's poor marriage was known the uncles were displeased but the bad match was forgiven.

Benjamin Langlois, who was to survive his brothers, took a great liking to his nephews 'and took his duties as self-appointed guardian, mentor and paymaster of his nephews and their children very seriously'. But in his great-nephew Thomas Langlois, the first-born son of Anthony Peter, Benjamin took a personal interest. The young man had to follow classical studies, take exercise and fence, and of course go to University. 'Since he held the money bags his advice was virtually command.'

In 1791 letters were exchanged between uncle Benjamin Langlois and Col. Lefroy, Tom's father, expressing concern about young Tom's state of health and weak eyesight. From other sources we know that it was decided that a holiday in Hampshire at the home of his uncle — the Rev. Isaac Peter George Lefroy of Ashe — would restore Tom to health.

But the reader of the Memoir of Chief Justice Lefroy will find no mention of this holiday. This omission has only one explanation: mentioning the Hampshire period the author of the Memoir had also to mention the relationship with Jane Austen, which would have added to its interest. Had this relationship been a youthful love affair as is unanimously accepted, he would, no doubt, have mentioned it. But this being contrary to the truth he refused to do so.

To write the truth — that Jane Austen has been the great, life-long love of his father he could not do either, out of respect for the memory of his mother. So Thomas Lefroy Junior chose to be silent on the Hampshire episode and the name of Jane Austen is never mentioned in the Memoir.

But one thing should be emphasized: both Jane Austen's and Thomas Lefroy's life stories have been consigned by close family members in two Memoirs, published at about the same time, respectively in 1869 and 1871. So that we may wonder and dream.

I propose to quote here a few passages from the address which young Tom Lefroy delivered at the opening of the Historical Society, in 1795. His brilliant mind, ease and clarity of expression and maturity of thought are exceptional at such an early age — he was eighteen. It is easy to understand that his family had the greatest expectations for his further career in life.

December 20, 1794

Mr Lefroy was elected Auditor at the opening of the second session of the revived Historical Society, and on the 28th of October, 1795, delivered the following address:

TRINITY COLLEGE, FROM COLLEGE GREEN, DUBLIN

Reproduced from G. N. Wright: *Ireland Illustrated*, London 1831, by courtesy of Trinity College Library, Dublin.

'Gentlemen of the Historical Society, — I congratulate you that we are re-assembled at our post — not a second time to found our Institution, but certainly to found the era of its stability. We may now lay aside all those anxieties and apprehensions by which we were surrounded in our previous course, henceforward to advance with the cheerfulness and hope of an assured existence. We are re-assembled, I trust, not relaxed in a single nerve of our zeal, but strengthened and confirmed in the spirit of persevering resolution. The very circumstance of our meeting together in this University, and our being drawn closer together here, suggests sentiments congenial and favourable to the task we are about to engage in. If we but a little anticipate the scenes of life to which we ourselves shall be differently called, in these we shall find that much of what experience prompts us to admire, has received its first culture in the exercises which this Institution holds forth to our acceptance. The knowledge of man and his nature in all the varieties which history exhibits must be for ever interesting and instructive. The embellishments of composition are called for by the refinement of literary taste, but above all here is laid a foundation for that persuasive art which is alone adequate to speak its own praises and its supreme influence over mankind...' (Thomas Lefroy, *Memoir of Chief Justice Lefroy*, by his son, Thomas Lefroy, Dublin, 1871 pp.402–3)

'...Important, however, as the cultivation of history undoubtedly is, serviceable as the lessons of it may prove which are here impressed on the early memory, we should yet have seen but a few and perhaps the most inconsiderable benefits of this Institution were we to rest here. I do not hesitate to point out here as a still greater advantage of our Society the opportunity it affords of cultivating public speaking. Perhaps there are some who would differ from me on this point. Of such I would ask, whether, of all the faculties with which nature has endowed us, is one alone to be left to grow wild? Is the art of public speaking, is oratory — and oratory alone — incapable or unworthy of cultivation and improvement? No. I am persuaded that in this, as in every other faculty of our nature, excellence is to be attained by slow and painful toil...' (*Ibid.* pp.404–5)

'...Clearness and precision of expression are indispensable rules to be observed by him who desires to attain any eminence as a public speaker. They are improvements in style towards which every man may and ought to make some progress. So necessary is the art of expressing our thoughts with clearness and precision, and so essential to the useful exercise of our other faculties, that without some degree of it we shall find the noblest of them, which is reason, to be miserably maimed and defective.' (*Ibid.* p.406)

'...But Gentlemen, I have detained you too long — too long for your patience, too long for my own capacity, too long for everything but my own gratification in addressing a Society to which I feel my affections so linked, from which I believe no ordinary pursuit or pleasure, nothing but the urgent voice of an arduous and honourable calling, should induce me to separate myself, even for a while; but I trust that at no period, in no situation, however occupying or engrossing, shall I forget what I owe to this Institution. At all times shall I be glad to lay at its feet the feeble offering of my exertions; at all times shall I be mindful and proud to boast of the honours it has thought fit to confer on me, but more especially of this last and most distinguished mark of its regard. May the same zeal which has so wonderfully matured this Society to what it is, still speed you in your course, and all through life animate your pursuit of virtue, learning, and honest fame.' 'Thomas L. Lefroy' (*Ibid.* p.416)

With this 'prehistory' in mind we can perhaps better understand that the Lefroy family from Ashe was very anxious about confronting uncle Benjamin with a new 'imprudent alliance' with a penniless girl, daughter of an obscure village clergyman, and this while young Tom was under their charge and responsibility as a guest in Hampshire.

The story of the short romance and its abrupt ending has been told in noble words — partly by Jane herself in her first and last novels, the happy endings belonging only to fiction — and partly by her biographers.

We know what Jane made of her life: how 'an inward treasure' born with her kept her alive through the years of sorrow after Tom's departure, and helped her in the far from easy life of a poor, unmarried relative.

Miss Austen from Chawton, the dutiful daughter, the affectionate sister and loving aunt, so unobtrusive, unknown to most of her readers, was to be celebrated after her death. She was to be compared with the greatest among the great. 'Her portrayals are so accurate and clear that her works have become tests of truth in Western culture, refreshing and clarifying us as deeply as Dante, Cervantes or Shakespeare may.' (Park Honan, *Jane Austen: Her Life*, Weidenfeld and Nicolson, 1987 p.403)

Jane Austen has been compared with Mozart because of 'unexampled mastery of symmetry, balance, clarity and restraint... each of them is often held up as the purest example of the classical equilibrium...'

Parallels have been drawn between Jane Austen's novels and Mozart's piano concertos — in which we find 'the exquisite balance between the one and the many or solo and orchestra'. (Robert K. Wallace, *Jane Austen and Mozart — Classical Equilibrium in Fiction and Music*, The University of Georgia Press, Athens, 1983 pp.2–8)

Most interesting for us at this point is the statement that: 'Mozart refused to accept that tragedy was there'. This statement is also valid for Jane Austen. In her personal life she had suffered grief and had been confronted with evil that had its origin in the callousness of the human heart. Nevertheless she wrote as if tragedy did not exist. She expressed this with her own words which have become famous: 'Let other pens dwell on guilt and misery. I quit such odious subjects as soon as I can, impatient to restore everybody not greatly in fault themselves, to tolerable comfort and have done with all the rest.' (*Mansfield Park*, Penguin, 1986, p.446)

That 'inward treasure born with her' made her avoid the abyss of evil and despair, directing her attention towards the sunny and only slightly cloudy aspects of life.

We know that she maintained her enthusiasm, her curiosity of mind and her sparkling wit, the passion and the patience to write her brilliant novels. And we know also, thanks to a thin red thread which here and there appears in her novels, as a hidden message for the attentive reader, that the balanced, amiable, cheerful woman had a secret: deep in her heart the great love of her youth was still alive.

But I often wondered what became of Tom Lefroy? Information was scarce. He went to practise at the Bar in Ireland. In 1799 he married Mary Paul, the sister of Tom Paul, a college friend. Helen Lefroy in the above-mentioned article wrote that 'the marriage was a singularly happy one'. Ten children were born and they all lived happily ever after...

But I still wonder. How was it possible that the young man described by his tutor at Trinity College, Dublin, Dr Burrowes, as a 'dutiful boy, with such a kind disposition and affectionate heart' could have behaved as he did towards Jane? How could he have been happy with another woman and enjoy life while Jane suffered? I tried to imagine him on his wedding day, leaving the church with his bride on his arm, the bells ringing, the crowd acclaiming the young couple, wishing them happiness. What was in his mind? in his heart?

One explanation is possible: Tom Lefroy acted in order not to grieve and disappoint his uncle Benjamin Langlois, his benefactor, to whom he owed so much, out of a feeling of duty. As in the tragedies of Corneille, he had to struggle and to choose between his love and his duty — or what he was convinced to be his duty.

And duty vanquished — he thus let himself be convinced to give Jane up and to be 'hurried away' without even saying farewell to the girl with whom he was deeply in love and who loved him dearly, and knowing he was breaking her heart. They obliged him to behave abominably. He was never to forgive himself. For a sensitive young man the experience was atrocious. His religious faith was to support him.

Towards the end of Jane Austen's last novel, *Persuasion*, there is a short sentence that shows that Jane was well aware that Tom Lefroy acted out a sense of duty towards his family. The words are pronounced after Anne Elliot and Frederick Wentworth are happily reunited. While talking, they analyse past events that led to their parting, and Anne says: 'When I yielded, I thought it was to duty.'[1] (Jane Austen, *Persuasion*, Penguin, 1986 p.246)

L'AIMABLE JANE (1801)
Reproduced by courtesy of the National Portrait Gallery, London.

Two coincidences are worth mentioning. The first is: In the biographical notice which he wrote for the posthumous edition of *Northanger Abbey* and *Persuasion* Henry Austen, describing his sister quoted John Donne: 'her eloquent blood spoke through her modest cheek.' And with nearly the same words Sophia Western, Tom Jones' great love is described: 'her pure and eloquent blood spoke in her cheeks...' though Henry Fielding mentioned John Donne. (Henry Fielding, *Tom Jones*, Penguin, 1972 p.352)

The second is: In *Persuasion* we come to know that the woman Captain Wentworth would marry should have 'a strong mind with sweetness of manners'. Anne Elliot possessed these qualities and so did Sophia Western, who 'with all the gentleness which a woman can have, had all the spirit which she ought to have.' (Henry Fielding, *Tom Jones*, Penguin, 1972 p.498)

These are indeed the very words that Tom Lefroy would have pronounced had he ever met Jane again. The 'dutiful boy' so well described by his tutor at Trinity College, had yielded to what he thought was his duty. And Jane understood and forgave him. She knew how dear she was to Tom and how he must have suffered. That knowledge, in spite of great sorrow, made her burden lighter than his.

Reader, let us for a moment dream that Sir Charles Grandison — the most kind and generous character fiction has ever created — had come to know about Tom Lefroy's great dilemma. As he never could hear about somebody being in need without coming to rescue, no doubt he would have personally provided in order to make Jane an eligible young girl or he would have succeeded to untie the purses of Jane's wealthy relatives: her brother Edward Knight, her aunt Mrs Leigh-Perrot.

But such characters appear at the right moment only in fiction and very seldom in real life. So Tom Lefroy was left to solve his problems alone.

From this crisis he emerged a changed, different person. The new person Tom Lefroy had become emerges between the lines of the article written by a descendant of the Lefroy family, Colonel J. A. P. Lefroy: 'Jane Austen's Irish Friend: Rt. Hon. Thomas Langlois Lefroy (1776–1869)', (Huguenot Society Proceedings, 1979, London).

It was with a shock that I 'met' the austere, grave and severe man that Thomas Lefroy had become — very religious and Calvinistic. His Calvinistic ideas were to increase with age. The change is heart-rending when we remember his miniature portrait representing a young man with a sweet smile, a loving expression in his eyes. And in Jane Austen's youthful letters we read about their profligate and shocking behaviour, about enjoyable evenings, dancing and attending balls.

The new person, the man who married Mary Paul, seems to have for ever forgotten how to enjoy life. From now on, to live will mean, for Thomas, doing his duty — as a man and as a Christian, towards his wife and his children, towards society and his country. Throughout his life one feature will be predominant: the austerity and the gravity of a man who has suffered a great loss, whose heart has been broken and shut for the pleasures of the world.

We may presume, and it is likely to have happened, that he read Jane's novels: they were in all hands, in all families. Elizabeth Bennet with her 'lively, playful disposition, which delighted in anything ridiculous', Anne Elliot's strong mind and gentle manner will be with him till the end of his life. Calling his first daughter, born in 1802, Jane, will never allow him to forget. There was, after all, to be a Jane Lefroy...

As a Christian he accepted this heavy burden. With all his energy he threw himself into the most varied battles and activities, in his profession and in politics.

The fact that Tom Lefroy married so soon after breaking with Jane was the wise decision of a practical young man. Since she was a sister of his College friend, Tom Paul, he must have known Mary for many years and he must have been sure that she would be an affectionate wife and a devoted mother. It was all that he needed. In fact Mary Paul was 'not at all intellectual but a sympathetic, loving, out-going person'. And they became engaged.

Tom had chosen well: Mary Paul was indeed wise, kind-hearted and had a strong Christian faith. She fulfilled her husband's expectations.

After thirty-six years of married life he could write to her: 'Often I thought what a blessing for time as well as for eternity is a union which has for its foundation the basis of religion.' (Thomas Lefroy, *Memoir of Chief Justice Lefroy*, by his son, Thomas Lefroy, Dublin, 1871, p.197)

His restlessness was very soon to manifest itself. 'Typically Thomas was not satisfied with the state of his legal knowledge when called to the Bar and after he became engaged he returned to London for further study while Mary stayed behind in her parents' house in Waterford.' After his marriage and the birth of some of his children, Thomas went to the Munster Circuit, leaving his family behind.

His absences were often long. He had to delay his dates for returning, to apologize — he wrote letters, received letters — was delighted with the accounts Mary gave him of his children. In a letter he asks his wife: 'Tell dear Anthony [his eldest son aged about seven years] how pleased I am to hear of his reading prayers for me every morning. Make him understand what he is about and learn him to pray from his dear little heart and not from his lips only.'

And to his daughter Jane, in a letter for Christmas (apparently sometimes he did not spend Christmas with his family) he wrote: 'Believe me, my darling girl, there is no progress to be made in anything without steady and continued application. A saunterer when young continues a saunterer through life.'

Here we have the grave, moralizing, preaching father whom his son later remembered. That a tendency for teaching and moralizing was already present in young Tom Lefroy is evident from some passages in *Northanger Abbey* and *Persuasion*. Here is one example from *Northanger Abbey*.

After Catherine Morland told Henry Tilney that she had learned to love a hyacinth he praised her:

> 'But now you love a hyacinth. So much the better. You have gained a new source of enjoyment, and it is well to have as many holds upon happiness as possible. Besides, a taste for flowers is always desirable in your sex, as means of getting out of doors, and tempting you to more frequent exercise than you would otherwise take... At any rate, however, I am pleased that you have learned to love a hyacinth. The mere habit of learning to love is the thing; and teachableness of disposition in a young lady is a great blessing.' (Jane Austen, *Northanger Abbey*, Penguin, 1987 p.179)

And also this passage from *Persuasion* where in chapter X Captain Wentworth catching a hazel-nut said to Louisa Musgrove:

'Here is a nut ... To exemplify, — a beautiful glossy nut, which blessed with original strength, has outlived all the storms of autumn. Not a puncture, not a weak spot any where. — This nut,' he continued with playful solemnity, — 'while so many of its brethren have fallen and been trodden under foot, is still in possession of all the happiness that a hazel-nut can be supposed capable of.' Then, returning to his former earnest tone: 'My first wish for all, whom I am interested in, is that they should be firm.' (Jane Austen, *Persuasion*, Penguin, 1986 p.110)

Captain Wentworth is playful as well as solemn. But it is evident that his language has a preacher's tone. From this tendency to moralize, however, it is a far way to the severe, austere Calvinistic attitude which became Thomas Lefroy's second nature in later life.

Young Tom Lefroy was a serious person with strong moral principles which must strongly have appealed to Jane and made him even dearer to her. But his strong moral base and religious faith did not prevent him from being the elegant young man who chose his clothes with great care, and who had a marked preference for sophisticated coats — for example the white coat[2] he wore even in the morning and shocked the rather conventional tastes of his young girlfriend! With a keen eye Jane had understood her friend, and Henry Tilney was a clergyman!

Because I have referred to Tom Lefroy's white coats and to his admiration for Tom Jones I wish to quote a passage from Fielding's novel which will help to better understand Tom Lefroy's youthful admiration for the hero:

Mr Jones...was in reality, one of the handsomest young fellows in the world. His face, besides being the picture of health, had in it the most apparent marks of sweetness and good-nature. These qualities were indeed so characteristic in his countenance, that while the spirit and sensibility in his eyes, tho' they must have been perceived by an accurate observer, might have escaped the notice of the less discerning, so strongly was this good-nature painted in his look, that it was remarked by almost everyone who saw him. (Henry Fielding: *Tom Jones*, Penguin, 1972, p.453)

In his article about 'Jane Austen's Irish Friend' the author underlines his religious convictions. So we read:

His religious convictions had always been very strong, and as he matured, his ideas became increasingly Calvinistic in character... It is unfortunate that the official Memoir of him, written by his son, dwells almost exclusively on his personal moral and religious attitudes and experience. There is no doubt that his religious conviction was the great principle by which his opinions, utterances and actions were guided. Such was the man — but it is a great pity that because of exclusive concentration on this aspect, very little of his humanity has been bequeathed to posterity. (J. A. P. Lefroy, 'Jane Austen's Irish Friend' Proceedings of the Huguenot Society of London, 1979, pp.148–165)

This is very strange indeed as a family with ten children might have provided many memories of pleasant moments spent with their father — birthday parties, balls, theatricals, funny or moving circumstances of a happy family life. But very little is said. This silence evokes a peculiarly austere atmosphere, a Calvinistic household where there was little time for fun or — country dances. Life was to be taken seriously. And very seriously he took it, Thomas's activities reached far beyond his juridical profession.

I happened to find out that one of Thomas Lefroy's sons had written a Memoir about his father and I made efforts to obtain the *Memoir of Chief Justice Lefroy*, by his son Thomas Lefroy. I succeeded, and of all places, it was the Old Library of Trinity College, Dublin, which supplied me with the microfilm of the book.

Before continuing I wish to warn the reader of the very special character of the *Memoir*. Working as a young lawyer on the Circuit, being MP for Trinity College and Chief Justice of Ireland in later years, Thomas Lefroy was spending frequent and long periods away from home. To keep in contact with his family he wrote letters, many letters. This explains why the *Memoir* mainly consists of letters dating from different periods of his life: letters addressed to his young wife, to his young children — but also letters written in later years to his wife, adult children, to his aged father.

Again I wish to warn the modern reader, AD 1995, of the very special character of these letters. World literature abounds in published correspondences; their contents being varied as life itself, treating small or important events, with comments on art and politics, places, books and people. Also personal experiences. But the reader of the *Memoir of Chief Justice Lefroy* will encounter none of these usual topics.

There are only two great subjects which are treated in all of Thomas Lefroy's letters dating from all periods of his life: religion and morale.

The reason why I thought it necessary to reproduce so many letters was to show that he never changed. All his letters contain only comments on the books he was reading, mainly the Gospels, St Paul's epistles, different commentaries of the Holy Scriptures and his own commentaries and meditations. Brief mention is made by the author of the *Memoir* of events — private and professional, but the *Memoir* mainly consists of letters.

Without knowing Thomas Lefroy's life the reader of the *Memoir* would be very amazed indeed, for which young man would write such letters to his young wife or to his young children? There is only one explanation: the only way to avoid memories dear and painful, regrets and remorse to haunt his thoughts was to occupy his mind permanently, when not busy with professional problems, with the study of the Holy Scriptures. It was the only way to regain and maintain his peace of mind. He was to persevere all his life.

Reader, I wish also to apologize for the long quotations, I feel they are necessary as a moving evidence of how deep the wound and how lasting grief have been.

All my efforts were rewarded. In reading the Memoir I obtained a deeper insight into the new person whom Tom Lefroy had become. And, thanks to the many letters he wrote to his wife and children, reproduced in the Memoir, I gained an understanding of his relationship with them. Most impressive was the knowledge I acquired of the intensity of his religious faith: his permanent preoccupation in every moment of leisure — even when he was travelling by coach — with the Holy Scriptures and the Epistles of St Paul. He was always reading, comparing, meditating...

In all the letters addressed to his wife, there emerges between the lines a tremendous and permanent need of support, help and guidance in the acceptance of God's will: a permanent need to listen to the voice which rises from the holy texts, soothing, encouraging, teaching, 'bringing pardon, peace and love'.

The following is dated from Mountrath, on his journey to join the Munster Circuit, in 1810:

To His Wife

Mountrath, Friday night,

I put a few lines into the Maryboro' post about 4 o'clock, but lest by any accident you should not get them I send this letter to Mr Bourne, the coach proprietor, with a request that he may forward it to you, as no post goes into town on Sunday, when it will arrive. We have had a fine though rather dull day, the coach not full, so that I had plenty of leisure and inclination for reading. I spent my day in preparing for Dunne* for the long vacation. I read over and compared most part of the Epistle to the Romans, with all those to the Galatians and the Ephesians, and part of those to the Corinthians; every time I read and compare them new light breaks in, and I am determined I will work on without note or comment endeavouring to make out the meaning for myself, which I should think may be done by patience and attention. By taking advantage of all the moments which would otherwise go to waste, great progress may be made in this undertaking besides the new portion of life which it infuses into the work which ought always to be going on within — of detecting the lurking-places of sin and the disguises of selfishness and purifying of the heart. These are, I am sure,

---

* He alludes to the Rev. James Dunne, an eminent clergyman of that day, with whom he passed much time in the long vacations, and had many discussions on Scriptural subjects.

the true and primary objects with a view to which we ought to read the Scriptures; but I think these will be greatly aided, when we understand all the bearings and connexion of the several parts of Scripture. There is another great good which results from applying even the shreds and patches of times in this way. It serves to allay somewhat the high relish and excitement which this world and all its pursuits and objects are hourly forcing on the imagination and the heart; it keeps in our view a glimpse, at least, of the true in opposition to the glare of the false treasure which we are for ever pursuing, and between the legitimate and excessive pursuit of which the bounds are so treacherous. I include under the head of false treasure every object of earthly attachment however innocent or even praiseworthy, on which a value is set beyond what any earthly object is entitled to, and yet this is a point upon which we are all most sadly and practically going astray every hour of our lives, and on which nothing can set us right but keeping before us, as if in a magnifying glass, the great and paramount claims to a Christian's regard. (Thomas Lefroy, *Memoir of Chief Justice Lefroy*, by his son, Thomas Lefroy, Dublin, 1871 pp.28–9).

To His Daughter J—

Limerick, Monday.

My Darling J—, Your letter gave me great pleasure; it was fairly written, well worded and no mistakes in the spelling; and I hope, by employing your time regularly between this and the next time I leave home, you'll be able to correspond with me on subjects of more importance. Believe me, my darling girl, there is no progress to be made in anything without steady and continued application, which, besides the advantages it brings in the way of improvement, makes labour pleasant from habit instead of being irksome, as it always is to the idle and irresolute. A saunterer when young, continues a saunterer through life. Nothing has always struck me so forcibly to show the value of order, and precision in our works, as observing the regularity and exactness displayed in all the works of God, day and night — summer, winter, autumn, and spring, — the regular and uniform motions of the almost infinite host of heavenly bodies. In the same manner in His Kingdom of grace, there is a time and a season for everything. Although a thousand years are in his sight as one day, nothing is permitted to occur a moment before its appointed time. Our blessed Lord's constant observation was, 'mine hour is not yet come'. How is it possible that we can expect to please God in the neglect of order and the disregard of stated times for different purposes? Indeed the event shows it, for He appears in an eminent degree to send a blessing upon diligence and industry in every situation of life, and these are necessarily connected with a regard to time and order. As I am satisfied my darling J— has real delight in pleasing me, I thought I could not do better than tell her a principal mode of doing so, and what is done from a sense of duty to a Father in heaven as well as to a father on earth, must yield happiness and improvement.

My dearest J—'s
Truly affectionate father, T. L.

(Ibid. pp.31–2)

To His Son A—

I hope you are a faithful chaplain, and make them all attend regularly at prayers during my absence, and that you recollect that to pray as we ought is not merely to repeat words, and to be thinking of something else, we must recollect what it is we are going about, and in whose presence we kneel down, and that He sees our hearts and minds as plainly as we see one another, and that He regards only prayer that comes from the heart, and in which the mind is engaged. I hope you are attentive to your business, and get your lessons, not merely so as to pass, but so as to understand them as perfectly as you can, and above all things that you don't loiter and waste time. When you play, — play, — but when you read, read and don't play. God bless you, my darling boy.

Your ever affectionate father, T. L.

(Ibid. p.33)

To His Daughter A—

I hope you are very attentive, and that you will have your chapter* as well as usual on my return. Mind whatever your darling mamma and Miss Clarke say to you, and papa will love you always. (Ibid. pp.33–4)

* During our childhood we used to meet together in his study every Sunday, having read and prepared for examination a chapter in one of the four Gospels; one Sunday he saw me playing about at the time I ought to have been preparing my chapter, and on his remonstrating with me, I said in a very hasty temper, 'It is too bad to have all lessons and no play even on Sunday,' when he drew me towards him in the most affectionate and patient manner and said 'Do you forget, dear T —, what David says, "In thy presence is fullness of joy; at thy right hand are pleasures for evermore." (Ps.XVI, II). Now though we cannot while here have this fullness of joy that we shall have hereafter in God's presence, yet, believe me, even in this world, there is no pleasure half so real or so lasting as is to be found in the reading and meditating upon His Word, if we will only receive it, and rest

And at a subsequent assizes he writes the following letter to be received by his children on Good Friday:

Limerick, Wednesday.

My Darling Children, You will receive this letter on the most wonderful day that comes in the course of the whole year, and as God has been good and gracious in affording you this knowledge, I am anxious, if I can, to lead you to spend it as becomes those who know its value. It was on this day that our Saviour, Jesus Christ, died on the cross, to the end, that all who believe on Him should not perish, but have everlasting life. Let us ask ourselves, not giddily, but with thought and seriousness, what could have induced Him to do this for us, or why should God have required it. The answer to the first question is very plain — it could have been only love to man that could have induced Him to leave the glory and happiness He had with the Father, and to take our nature and suffer all He did whilst on earth; but see what ought to be the consequence of this if we have one spark of gratitude in our heart. Ought it not to be as St Paul says, that we ought not henceforth to live unto ourselves, but unto Him who loved us and gave Himself for us. If you feel it right because your parents are kind and love you, to love them in return, and to study to please them, and to do what they desire (and no doubt it is so), how infinitely greater is the obligation to Him who laid down His life for you, who bore to be mocked and tortured and nailed to a cross that you and I and all who will come to Him may escape the misery and the torture of hell. But consider further, and this leads me to answer the second question — what was the cause of all this? It was sin, and until we know what sin is, we know nothing. Sin is a worse disorder of the soul than putrefying sores are to the body; it is worse to the soul than the most malignant fever to the body. Sin can no more dwell in the presence of God than darkness can dwell with light; sin is misery in the end, and its wages is death, — and even in this life don't we find that there is no peace to the wicked, but that they are like the troubled sea, casting up mire and sand. What then ought we to think — how ought we to feel towards Him who came to cure the soul of man and to set it free from the curse of sin. What would you say to the physician that cured your body and restored you from pain to live even a few years longer in this poor world? What then ought to be our thoughts of Jesus Christ who came to cure our

our souls upon it as the word of Him who cannot lie.' I fear my reception of his beautiful and affectionate remonstrance could have afforded him but little comfort, as I remember turning away from him certainly more in a sulky than a grateful mood, but the impression was never effaced from my mind. Often and often in after years when I sat down to my Bible, his sweet counsel came back to my recollection with an influence and pleasure which my original reception of it could but little have led the fond and loving counsellor to expect. (Thomas Lefroy, *Memoir of Chief Justice Lefroy* Dublin, 1871) never-dying souls from the disorder of sin, so terrible in its effects that the language used to express them is that which describes the most dreadful suffering we know of — burning by fire. But the worst of sin still remains to be told — it makes us insensible to itself. It makes us blind to our own faults, it even makes us fancy ourselves what we are not, till at length we become, as the Bible says, dead in sin — that is, as insensible of our sinfulness as a dead body is of feeling. It blinds, it hardens, it palsies the soul of man. But the blessed Jesus came to cure this; whilst upon earth He gave sight to the blind, and feet to the lame, and power to the decrepit and palsied — as a proof that He could and would also cure the like disorders of the soul for all who come to Him with the same faith and trust as these sick people did — of all of whom you may remember it is said that *Jesus seeing their faith healed them*. How then are we to come to Him? By coming to His own Book the Bible — by believing and receiving and thinking often upon what we there read; by having Him always in view, considering whether what we are doing, saying, or thinking would please Him; by praying for His instruction, that He would send His Holy Spirit into our hearts to make us sensible of their sinfulness, to make us hate sin, and desire as the greatest of all blessings to be delivered from it; to feel love and gratitude for all His love and tenderness; to think often what He has done and suffered for us, and to remember every day in the year this wonderful day on which the Son of God died for sinful rebellious man, bore the punishment we deserve, and procured for us the pardon we stood so much in need of, and the life, and joy, and peace for evermore which God alone can give.

May we so receive all His blessings, my darling children, that they may not turn to judgment against us.

Your ever affectionate father, T. L.

(*Ibid.* pp.35–6)

The following bears the postmark of Waterford July, 1812.

To His Wife

I arrived here yesterday about five o'clock from Kilkenny where I completed all my business. It rained in the night, but the day took up about eleven o'clock; and so fresh was the air, so lively and beautiful all the scene from Kilkenny to Ballyheale, that I was quite in a '*Wicklow trance*'* all the way. To see the blessings of heaven so profusely poured out as far as the

---

* This was a household word in our family circle from the great admiration he had for the scenery of the County Wicklow where for many years he spent his summer vacations.

eye could reach without a single damaged ear of corn after the threatened danger of a famine, with the sun suddenly breaking out and enlivening the whole scene, made me exclaim as I reached the top of one of those fine hills, How excellent are Thy works, Oh Lord; in wisdom hast Thou made them all. Oh make me to see and feel in this goodly scene of joy and gladness the sure pledge of that greater glory, though yet unseen, which Thou hast prepared for those that love and serve Thee; and give me in the contemplation of Thy invisible mercies the same delight I received in this manifestation of Thy power and goodness. How I longed to have you with me and all our dear babes about us, as we had on our last Wicklow excursion. But a moment's reflection in that mood served to banish all repinings. If it be necessary that we should be separated for a while, we are still living together in His presence — protected by His power, and watched over by His mercy, whose goodness is over all; and, I think, our faith and dependence on Him would be but the profession of our lips if we suffer ourselves to doubt that in every dispensation which can or may occur, all takes place under His providence, and that all things work together for good (that is final real good) for those who love God. It is not place, or absence, or presence of friends, that does or can constitute our essential well-being; and whilst we are practically and sincerely persuaded of that great truth, we must and ought to repose with entire confidence on Him for the safety and protection of those we love — I mean their safety and protection in every sense in which these are permitted to be objects of a Christian's desire.

T. L.

To His Wife

Nenagh, 15th September

As no post left this last night I could not give you any earlier account of our arrival. We had, though a wet morning, a very pleasant day, and from our very gratifying and I trust profitable conversation and reading we rejoiced that a post chaise and not the coach, was our vehicle. Mr and Mrs Bennet received us in the most cordial and friendly manner. I have written to my County Limerick tenants to meet me in Limerick on Wednesday, so that I expect to return here on Thursday, and to be home, please God, either Friday or Saturday. We have been at a retired but beautifully situated country church, where I was more surprised and delighted than I remember to have been for a long time. We had, from a coarse, weather-beaten old man, as sound, as affectionate, as earnest, and animating a Gospel sermon as I have almost ever heard — coming evidently from his own heart, and reaching ours. It was delightful to find, from enquiry, how (let the exterior be what it may) divine truth both purifies and softens the heart, for I find that he has been long valued and esteemed as a worthy, excellent man by those around, most of whom neither regarded nor admired him in the pulpit; but there he stood like a witness in the wilderness, testifying to all the glorious and animating hope which gilds and gladdens his own setting day. His text was, 'looking unto Jesus the author and finisher of our faith, who for the joy that was set before Him endured the cross, despising the shame, and is set down at the right hand of the throne of God'. May this be the polar star of our course — and the text written upon our hearts until it quickens into life and action. May He, who is the alone author and perfector of any good, accomplish in all of us this, His greatest blessing, giving us herein pardon, peace, and love.

T. L.

(Ibid. pp.40–1)

The following extracts from two letters, written to his wife in the year 1813, in relation to a disappointment he had met with, about a matter on which they were both very anxious, exhibit the earnestness of his desire that complete submission to God's will should be made the ruling principle in his own heart, and the hearts of those he loved; and also the peace of mind which even then he enjoyed from 'cherishing the habit' — to use his own words — of following the path of duty and leaving results to God.

To His Wife

Waterford, Monday.

...But all things are for the best, and I hope we shall daily learn more and more so to think and feel. We should thus both have more of that perfect peace which they have, whose minds are stayed on God; doing our part, we should cherish the habit of being satisfied with the result, casting all our care on Him who careth for us, and knows and designs better things for us than we could do for ourselves. The comfort and security are inexpressible which result from no longer considering ourselves merely as our own, depending on our own puny strength or foresight, but as objects of Almighty care and love. 'He that spared not His own Son, but delivered him up for us all, how shall He not with him also freely give us all things?' This is plainly unanswerable, if we believe the first part; but there is the sticking point of unbelief; we really do not (as we ought) deeply, fully, and without any reserve, believe that amazing truth, that the Great God of the Universe gave the Son of His love to die for man, a poor worm of the earth. If we believed this as we ought, there is nothing too merciful, too tender, to be expected from love like this. This is the great truth which should therefore be ever present to our hearts. This is the bright and morning star, which will light and guide us on our way through this maze of ignorance and sin. The hearty reception and deep persuasion of this is what St Paul alludes to as the object of his unceasing labour and striving, if he might by any means 'win Christ and be found in him.' From this, as from the sun in the centre of the system, result steadiness in our course, obedience to the laws of our Creator, light to guide us on our way, warmth to cheer and animate our progress, and love and joy and hope to confer all of happiness which the present scene allows.

For what reason do I dwell on this? It is, that we may labour whilst we are apart in seeking after the knowledge of our Lord and Saviour Jesus Christ, and praying to be led of God by His Holy Spirit to this knowledge — for thus we shall come together again for good. Thus shall our union be one which will endure when time shall be no more. I wish we may all think deeply and constantly on these things. Words are very light, easily written, easily read, easily forgotten, and we cannot too soon or too young begin the habit of dwelling on their import and full meaning, especially when they are the words of God. I wish my darling children, especially the older ones, would do this; a few sentences, read and reflected on, are more than chapters or volumes hastily and heedlessly gone over. It is with the soul as with the body, the food taken in must be digested in order to profit us.

T. L..
(Ibid. pp.41–3)

From early youth Thomas Lefroy had a taste for gardening. It is interesting to remember how approvingly Henry Tilney spoke about love of flowers, implying love of gardening in general 'as means of getting out of doors, and tempting you to more frequent exercise than you would otherwise take'. (Jane Austen, *Northanger Abbey*, Penguin, 1987 p. 179)

In later years, after his marriage, he indulged in gardening, encouraging the whole family to join him. His son Thomas remembers:

I have still vividly before me our whole merry-hearted group — parents and children sallying forth into the garden after dinner, the youngest as well as the oldest taking share in the busy task of weeding borders, watering flowers, cutting shreds, or sitting at his side while he pruned the fruit-trees, and reading the pretty story book which he had bought on his way from Court in order that the evening might not pass without profit as well as pleasure. He soon acquired such a practical knowledge and skill in gardening that he more than once carried off prizes at the Horticultural Shows from the proprietors of all the suburban villas, many of whom were admittedly amongst the first class of practical amateur gardeners.

(Ibid. p. 52)

This is the only occasion mentioned — from early years — of cheerful moments spent by the family together.

His strong religious faith was to be his support through all his life. I shall reproduce some letters written to his father, in later years, which all testify to his infallible confidence in the Word of God. Very interesting is a letter written in 1818 in which he warns against the dangers of the fashionable world. Very moving are also the letters written to his son Jeffry after he took holy orders, showing the same permanent interest in the study of the Holy Scriptures, as a guide in all circumstances of life.

Leeson Street, 21st April, 1817

My Dear Father I am indeed sincerely grieved to hear of your sufferings since I left you, and I wish with all my heart I could suggest anything for your relief. God grant that Phoebe may be able in her next to give me a better account of your chest and side. I heard yesterday from Robert Daly — one of our best men and best ministers — a sermon which I often wished you could have heard. It was on that beautiful Psalm (the 23rd), 'The Lord is my shepherd, therefore can I lack nothing. He shall feed me in a green pasture and lead me forth beside the waters of comfort.' After a very just and striking view of the extent of human affliction and observing that there was no promise even to the most favoured children of God that they should be exempt from these trials, he called our attention to the promises of comfort and support under these trials which are given to all who make the Lord their shepherd, and look to Him with faith and patience. He introduced those pathetic and beautiful passages from our Saviour's addresses, in which He calls himself 'our Shepherd' and calls us His 'sheep' and says to Peter 'feed my lambs', language which it is impossible to suppose He would ever have used if He did not mean to excite cordial and confident trust. Daly also observed that the Christian has no promise of not being exposed to temptation and sin, but then he has the promise to which David alludes in this same Psalm, 'He shall convert my soul and bring me forth in the paths of righteousness for His name's sake. Yea though I walk through the valley of the shadow of death I will fear no evil, for thou art with me; thy rod and thy staff comfort me.' So that though the Christian whilst he has flesh and blood to contend with will have to struggle against temptation, he has a promise that that Saviour whom he loves and trusts will by degrees strengthen his soul so as to make the struggle less, and will as assuredly in the end procure for him pardon and peace; and all He asks is that we should believe in Him. Even should our faith be not so lively as we could wish He has compassion on our infirmities, He is touched with the feeling of them, and for that, as one gracious purpose, took our nature upon Him. Be of good cheer therefore my dearest father, though we are not to

HOUSE AND GARDEN OF A ROAD FARM, SURREY
We can imagine Thomas Lefroy or Henry Tilney gardening...

Reproduced from Lawrence Weaver: *Small Country Houses*, London 1914, by courtesy of the Rijksmuseum Stichting, Amsterdam.

put our trust in princes or in any son of man; we cannot too firmly trust to our God and Saviour. He was under no necessity to give us the assurance of His love, which He has done, and why doubt the utmost extent of what He has promised.

My dearest father's
Ever affectionate son, T. L.

(Ibid. 58–60)

Leeson Street, May 5, 1818

My Dear Father, ...It is true I passed by that part of your former letter which related to my not going to the Castle, but I deferred answering it only till I should have time to go fully into the subject. I confess to you I am afraid to be anywhere where duty does not call me, especially in scenes where there is a great deal to excite and inflame the pride of life; a man has no business to walk in slippery places if he is very anxious not to fall, and still more if he wishes to guard all those who are leaning on him from falling. I do not feel that if I frequented the Castle, and the line of society in which it would necessarily involve me, that I could consistently or reasonably expect our children hereafter to keep out of that mischievous round of worldly and frivolous pleasures so utterly inconsistent with the sobermindedness and purity of the Christian character. I see and know how many men in my own profession have had their sons ruined, their expectations blasted, and their talents perverted from usefulness by the example and influence of the society they have been led into by frequenting the scenes I am afraid to enter into. I do not say that a Christian cannot or ought not to go to the Castle; he may go there or anywhere if his lawful calling and duty bring him there, but I don't feel that mine do. I went when it was proper, to return thanks; and if I should again have a like occasion to go there, I shall not fear to go in discharge of duty. These are the short reasons for my declining to make one of the gay or fashionable world; not that I dislike gaiety, for in truth I believe I enjoy more of it than those who seek it in these scenes. All at home join in love with my dear father's

Ever affectionate and dutiful son, T. L.

(Ibid. pp.64–5)

Do not the contents of this letter remind us of one of Jane Austen's characters, Sir Thomas Bertram of Mansfield Park who might himself have written it? Do not these lines express his very own partiality for a quiet, austere family life? Sir

Thomas never said it in so many words, but it is his children and Fanny Price who described the great austerity of their family life:

> 'I think', said Fanny, 'in my opinion Sir Thomas would not like *any* addition. I think he values the very quietness you speak of, and the repose of his own family circle is all he wants ... As well as I can recollect, it was always much the same. There never was much laughing in his presence ... I cannot recollect that our evenings ... were ever merry except when my uncle was in town.' (Jane Austen, *Mansfield Park*, Penguin, 1986 pp.211–2)

Is it not as if the silhouette of Thomas Lefroy is passing silently between the lines when Fanny Price, evoking Sir Thomas, described him 'as a fine looking man, with most gentleman-like, dignified, consistent manners ... his reserve, his powers may be a little repulsive.' (Jane Austen, *Mansfield Park*, Penguin, 1986 p.213) And is not Fanny Price an authentic, little Huguenot, even if she is pretty and often blushes?

Are we mistaken in considering *Mansfield Park* as a silent homage to her Irish friend? We must remember that *Mansfield Park* is the first novel that Jane Austen wrote in adult life, the first two published novels, *Sense and Sensibility* and *Pride and Prejudice* being youthful novels which she corrected and improved in later years.

Mansfield Park is above all a book about the difficulty of preserving true moral consciousness in the selfish manoeuvring of society. Jane Austen knew that to be virtuous was difficult, that much pain and effort are needed to maintain true values in a world of dangerous forces and power-play. Fanny Price stands for the difficulty of right thinking in a world of subtly corrupted instincts. She accepts tranquillity in a world where pleasure seems to lie in complete freedom and movement. She speaks for 'inner light' in a world of worldly standards. All so very actual and true today AD 1995...

After one has read the *Memoir of Chief Justice Lefroy*, after one has learned of Thomas Lefroy's lifelong struggle to maintain true values in a changing world, *Mansfield Park* — sometimes described as 'a strange book' — acquires a deeper meaning.

The following letters, selected from a correspondence carried on during his busiest periods in the House of Commons, with his son, the Reverend Jeffry Lefroy, soon after his son's entering into the ministry, give us an insight into the subjects on which his heart constantly dwelt, even in the midst of worldly engagements ever so engrossing, and show us something of the anxiety with which he sought to assist by his counsel, and guide by his experience, those who — to use his own words — 'were always in his thoughts':

House of Commons
Monday, March 11th 1833.

My Dearest Jeffry, I cannot let my first frank to your new address go without a line from myself, though, as you may suppose, very busy. But, whilst I feel the weight and thanklessness of my own labours, it rejoices me that my own dear Jeffry is engaged in a work which, whatever be its weight, from its importance, is the work of a gracious Master — a light burden and an easy yoke when the heart is in it, and the more it is so, the more easy and delightful the work becomes; but even the labour of this world is lightened by the sweet help which God's grace ministers, by enabling us to run with patience and hope the race that is set before us, with our eye and heart upon Him whose eye and heart, we know, are towards us. Dear —'s society is a great comfort, and, indeed, a spiritual blessing, as we are enabled to take sweet counsel together — in conversation, in reading, and prayer. Believe me, you are never forgotten in our prayers; may you know the reality of the power and blessedness of prayer, of persevering, believing prayer; may you know the reality and the power of the love of a gracious God manifested to us in His own dear Son; may you know the reality of the truth, 'that the Blood of Jesus Christ cleanseth from all sin'. Oh! what weapons will you then be furnished with to fight the battle of the Lord against the world, the flesh, and the devil. Dig incessantly in that mine of rich treasure, your Bible, so as to read it *with understanding*; that is, first, to ascertain what the Word says, and then to believe, fearless of consequences, but fearful only of putting man's wisdom in the place of God's. The Lord has blessed you with great help where you are, and I trust you will not fail to profit by it to the uttermost. Aim at nothing less than a full and clear understanding of the Scriptures, of the *whole* word of God, but don't be anxious or precipitate about systems — desire to drink in truth by degrees from the Fountain Head itself, as the Lord, the Spirit, gives it gradually to His babes in Christ — here a little, and there a little — but ever adding line upon line, precept upon precept, that you may be at length 'thoroughly furnished unto very good work'. By faith and perseverance, we inherit all the promises — amongst the rest, wisdom and knowledge in Divine things. May the Lord bless you, and lift up the light of His countenance upon you, and keep and guide you, is the fervent prayer of

Your ever affectionate father, T. L.

(Thomas Lefroy, *Memoir of Chief Justice Lefroy*, by his son, Thomas Lefroy, Dublin, 1871 pp.199–201)

I also reproduce a passage of Baron Lefroy's charge to the Grand Jury in the trial *The Queen* v. *John Mitchell*. This shows the deep humanity in his judicial work.

THOMAS LEFROY, LORD CHIEF JUSTICE OF IRELAND. JULY 30 1855

Reproduced by courtesy of the National Library of Ireland, Dublin.

> ...I have been somewhat withdrawn from the observations which I meant to have confined to your own case, by reference to a subject which I did not think I could avoid adverting to after what had passed yesterday. But to return to your own case. I wish you to understand that we have, with the utmost anxiety to arrive at a right decision upon the measure of punishment which it is our duty to impose, postponed passing the sentence until this morning. We have examined the case with great deliberation, and with great anxiety duly to discharge the duty we owe to the prisoner, of not awarding a punishment beyond the just measure of the offence; as well as the duty we owe to the Queen, and to the public, that the measure of punishment should be such as should carry with it the effect of all punishment, which is not the infliction of suffering upon the individual, but the prevention of crime — that the punishment should carry with it a security, as far as possible, to the country, that one who appeared so perseveringly and so deliberately a violator of the law, should not be permitted to continue the course he had entered upon for the disturbance of its peace and prosperity, and that the country should have time, if possible, to recover from the infliction which that course had imposed upon it. If this had not been the first adjudication upon the Act, we might have felt ourselves obliged to carry out its penalties to their utmost extent, but taking into consideration that this is the first adjudication, though the offence is as clearly proved, and is almost as enormous as it can be anticipated that any offence of the kind can be proved to be hereafter, the sentence of the Court is, that you be transported beyond the seas for the term of fourteen years.

The following extract from the letter of an eyewitness of the proceedings, represents, as I believe, the impression left on the minds of all who were engaged in or present at the trial.

> ...Mitchell's trial is over, and the Baron's most anxious friends could not desire more than the universal admiration elicited from men of all creeds and politics by the way in which he conducted the case. His dignity of demeanor, and his resolute firmness, blended with courtesy and patience throughout the whole of this difficult and important trial, were the subject of general observation. (*Ibid.* pp.274–5)

Towards the end of this Memoir, the author reveals aspects of the inner life of his father, his permanent interest in the study of the Bible, the importance of prayer in daily life.

> The feature of his character in private life, which was most generally observed by those who enjoyed an intimate acquaintance with him, was his love for the study of Scripture, and the tendency of his mind to lead

conversation to the discussion or consideration of Scriptural subjects; and, perhaps, in no way was the closeness of his walk with God so fully manifest, as in the happiness with which he looked forward to the Sunday, and the refreshment he always felt in the religious observances of the Lord's Day. No one who spent that day in his society could fail to observe that he regarded the sacred obligations of its religious duties, not as a tedious burden, but as a high and happy privilege. His earnest devotion in public worship told plainly that he was engaged in no mere form or ceremony, but was enjoying communion with his God; and with the exception of an hour or little more after church, during which he was in the habit of walking into the country with his children, the greater portion of the time which intervened between morning service and his dinner hour was spent in the retirement of his own study. But it was not on the Sabbath alone that he thus enjoyed holding communion with his God in private. He never travelled without having his Bible at hand, in his writing case, and, generally, some of Archbishop Leighton's works, or some book on Prophecy or on the Revelation, which formed the pastime of his journey. The following letter to his wife, giving an account of his journey from London, when returning from Parliament, in the bygone days of coach-travelling, well exemplifies this trait in his character:

Leeson Street,
Thursday.

We had, thank God, a delightful journey, and the weather in the Channel very fine until we approached Ireland, when it became wet and windy; but we made an excellent passage of six hours and a half. Robert Daly joined us at Birmingham; and from Shrewsbury he, Jeffry, and I had the coach wholly to ourselves, and so instructive and delightful a day I don't know when I passed. It is remarkable that I laid out the two days of this journey for going very minutely into the Prophecies which Lord Mandeville and I had been reading together, and I made it the subject of earnest prayer that I might be guided aright, and profit by my search. The first day I read through the whole journey, but was more than ever puzzled. However, I was so prepared by my reading to ask questions and receive instruction, that dear Robert Daly relieved me out of my chief perplexities and opened views of the subject so much more clear and satisfactory than any I had met with, that I consider myself to have had quite a gracious answer to my prayers. On landing, Daly came home with us for breakfast and read for us in our family worship. He is indeed a true servant of God. (*Ibid.* p.342)

The consistent witness of his daily walk to the reality of his Christian profession, hardly needs to be enlarged upon. Such frequent instances of it must crowd the memories of all who knew him. It may truly be said of him that he considered family prayer to be 'the border which keeps the web of daily life from unravelling'. When holding the first rank at the Chancery Bar, and overwhelmed with professional business, the duties of each day were opened and closed by assembling his whole household for family worship, consisting of a portion of Scripture which he read and accompanied with a few practical observations, concluding with prayer; and later in life when occupying a villa some miles distant from Dublin, he had daily to attend the Courts as Chief Justice, his morning hours were so regulated as to secure ample time for family worship before the departure of the train which carried him to his arduous and responsible duties. His habitual dependence on God's providence and love may be traced in his invariable practice of calling us all together for united prayer or thanksgiving on each occasion of separation or re-union. I do not recollect his ever leaving home to attend Parliament, or for his judicial duties on Circuit, without assembling the members of his family to ask for God's assistance and blessing upon the discharge of his own duties, and committing to his care and guidance those from whom he was parting.

To the inner circle of his family, and those who enjoyed the privilege of frequent intercourse with him, I feel that any memorial of him would be wanting which omitted to notice his unalterable cheerfulness under the little every-day crosses of life. Though the shadow of a cloud might flit past, it seemed as if it could never long obscure the sunshine of his temper or his countenance. (*Ibid.* p.369-70)

He never kept any diary, but he left behind him a large portfolio full of short notes on passages of Scripture and points of doctrine, jotted down from time to time as opportunity offered, and in these we have a clue to the topics which engaged his thoughts in his hours of retirement. From their dates they appear to have been commenced as early as 1816 and were carried on to 1860. I have selected some of these papers from the mass, as they are not without intrinsic value, and afford interesting evidences of his own practical experience as a Christian. (*Ibid.* p.342)

It is interesting and impressive to read that in the year 1816[3] a turning point took place in his spiritual life, that in that year Thomas Lefroy started to note down his thoughts after meditating on passages of the Scriptures. I shall reproduce some meditations from his Portfolio.

THE WAY APPOINTED BY GOD IS THE ONLY WAY OF SALVATION.

The moment I learn from the Most High how He chooses to be served, or to be glorified, there is an end to every suggestion of my own imagination as to any *other mode* of serving or glorifying Him. The answer to any other suggestion is, 'it may be very good,' your course *may* do well but I am sure of this one, because it is the mode appointed by Him who is to be served and glorified. When, therefore, God has appointed that He Himself is to be served and glorified, *by* serving and glorifying Christ as the appointed *medium* (the Mediator) by and through whom to serve and glorify God, we have nothing to do but to serve and glorify God, we have nothing to do but to accept entirely and heartily this method of serving and glorifying Him; let us leave to others their general speculations, but let it be our business to walk in the *appointed* path, and not to endeavour to find out a new or a better way. Christ is made unto us wisdom, sanctification, righteousness, and redemption — a *new* and *living* way for coming unto God. Let others take their own ways, and go on to find out other wisdom, other righteousness, and other sanctification; let us look only to *Jesus*, the author and finisher of our faith, the *appointed* Lamb, the *appointed* Redeemer, the *appointed* Sanctifier, *i.e.*, the medium by and through whom the Holy Spirit is granted — who has it in abundance to give; and let it be our study and prayer to find out His way and will, to follow His steps, and to keep His commandments, and to be, in all things, like unto Him. The daily watchword of the Christian should be, 'Looking unto Jesus'. (*Ibid.* p.345)

"DESIRE THE SINCERE MILK OF THE WORD THAT YE MAY GROW THEREBY." — 1 Peter ii. 2.

Mark the object the Apostle sets before us in his exhortation to desire the sincere milk of the word, *i.e.*, not for knowledge, but for spiritual growth, that thereby we may advance in spiritual growth. Until we feel and know by experience that Happiness is in proportion to Holiness, or in other words, in proportion to our conformity to Christ, we shall never rightly hunger and thirst after righteousness. But when the soul feels sin to be a disease, a misery, and feels conformity to the mind of Christ ... to be true happiness, then the soul begins to gasp like a parched and thirsty land for the dew of God's grace to give it of this delight, and to rescue it from its disease and from the burden of sin. They know nothing of the secret of the Lord — of the really divine life — who talk of crucifying the affections and lusts in order to come to Christ, and be partakers of his happiness. These must indeed be crucified that we may be partakers of His happiness, but it is He that must do it. No, no. Begin with winning Christ — Christ first, Christ second, Christ third, Christ to the end. Win Him — dwell in Him — get Him to dwell in the soul, and you'll see presently what will become of the affections and lusts that used to war against the soul. You'll see the temple cleansed, the oxen driven out, and the tables of the money changers overthrown, and these old marauders flying in all directions. A few more subtle than the rest will lurk behind, but they too shall be driven out in the end by the power of the Lord of the Temple. Come unto me, says Christ, all ye that are weary and heavy laden, and I will give you rest. This is the Gospel! 'By grace ye are saved through faith, and that not of yourselves.' (Ibid. pp.363-4)

In the Memoir, his son referred to the special bond of affection that had existed between Thomas Lefroy and his eldest daughter. One fact is *not* mentioned: that her name was *Jane*.

> ...His eldest daughter, whom he playfully called 'his guardian angel', was the constant companion of these daily rides; for from the time of our beloved mother's death in 1858, she was hardly ever separated from him even for a day, and with untiring watchfulness and forethought she seemed to anticipate every wish and provide for every want almost before it was felt by the loved object of her care. (Ibid. p.283)

The last days are evoked illness, suffering — but to the last Thomas Lefroy retained his cheerfulness, his humour. I shall make no comment but shall leave the attentive reader, who has a good memory, to remember,[4] **to compare**...

> To the last he retained a cheerful and patient endurance under suffering which often elicited the astonishment and admiration of those who attended upon him in sickness. I remember in his last illness (only two days before he was taken from us), after he had spent a very wearisome night from want of sleep, and great oppression of breathing, we closed the window-shutters in the morning, in the hope of his getting some sleep; just then the physician for whom an express had been sent, arrived from Dublin. After feeling his pulse, the doctor asked whether it would annoy him if the window-shutters were opened for a moment, when he replied with a cheerful smile 'not at all, doctor, I always like to have light thrown upon a subject'. (Ibid. p.386)

As already mentioned Thomas Lefroy's activities reached far beyond his juridical profession. He threw himself in the political struggle between Protestants and Catholics — a bitter strife then. He saw no good in Catholic emancipation, being convinced that a well-ordered system of education will be the remedy for the existing evil — the many crimes occurring in the violent conflict between Protestants and Catholics. Pleading with all his heart:

> I direct my observations to you as gentlemen who have schools on your estates. I would earnestly suggest the necessity for improving the present system of education, and see that the children are at least instructed in the fundamental truths of Christian religion.

Thomas himself took a deep interest in the 'Society for Promoting Education of the Poor of Ireland'. Suspicion and hostility of the Catholics opposed the success of this enterprise. In 1821 he became a founder and later Honorary Secretary of the 'Scripture Reader Society', whose object was to send Protestant missionaries into the traditional Roman Catholic areas.

It is also interesting to record that he was a life member and Vice President of the Irish Auxiliary to the Society for promoting Christianity among the Jews.

After the death of George IV in 1830 Thomas was invited by the Fellows of Trinity College to stand as Tory candidate for the University. Thomas sat in Parliament for eleven years. He had two great interests: Christian education and the 'Open Bible' in schools. He never really overcame his distaste for political life — although he took an active part in it, out of a feeling of duty no doubt...

In 1841 the Tories returned to power. Thomas confidently expected to be made Lord Chancellor of Ireland. But his sectarian views were well known and were an embarrassment to the Government. His expectations were unfounded. Reluctantly he accepted the post of Junior Baron of the Exchequer.

In 1848, the year of revolutions, the first State Trial of rebel leaders fell to the Rt. Hon. Baron Thomas Lefroy. His charge to the Grand Jury of the County of Dublin is a masterpiece of clear and able exposition of legal principles. (See p.71) In 1852 Lord Derby's administration made him Lord Chief Justice of Ireland. The gravity and courtesy of his demeanour was admired.

As years passed, he mellowed — he put off a great deal of the austerity of his creed — and avoided the tone of ascendant Protestantism. He was courteous to Catholic colleagues on the Bench, whom in his youth he had been taught to despise. He was to retain his high offices until the year of his death in 1869.

He worked impressively, retained all his faculties, rode daily the same horse as he had done for thirty years. He mellowed in the family circle, too. A life of hard labour, a life of fulfilled duty towards his large family and his country was ended.

There are some texts to which one feels specially attracted. One reads them again and again. Surrounded by a haze of mystery, it is as if by every new reading the veil is lifted a little more. It is evident that the author possesses a secret. It is also evident that he does not want to tell it. But the need to turn around, to suggest, to allude, is stronger than himself. A *Memoir* by James Edward Austen-Leigh is such a text.

With the exception of the short biographical note that Jane's brother Henry Austen wrote for the posthumous edition of *Northanger Abbey* and

Persuasion in 1818 and Caroline Austen's memoirs, *My Aunt Jane Austen* and *Reminiscences*, A Memoir is the only extensive text about Jane Austen written by somebody who had personally known her. James Edward has seen her and talked to her in her personal surroundings. He had known her sweet voice, her playfulness, her strong mind and gentle manner — remembering: 'We did not think of her as being clever, still less as being famous; but we valued her as one always kind, sympathising, and amusing.' This gives the text a special, moving charm.

But it is evident that James Edward knew more about the family history of the Austens than he was willing to reveal. One of the most moving passages is the evocation of Jane Austen's relationship to Tom Lefroy. It has become famous even if all that it conveys has not been completely understood. Here is the passage:

> At Ashe also Jane became acquainted with a member of the Lefroy family, who was still living when I began these memoirs, a few months ago: the Right Hon. Thomas Lefroy, late Chief Justice of Ireland. One must look back more than seventy years to reach the time when these two bright young persons were, for a short time, intimately acquainted with each other, and then separated on their several courses, never to meet again; both destined to attain some distinction in their different ways, one to survive the other for more than a half century, yet in his extreme old age to remember and speak, as he sometimes did, of his former companion, as one to be much admired, and not easily forgotten by those who had ever known her. (J. E. Austen-Leigh, *A Memoir*, Penguin 1986, pp.309–10)

I have read this passage many times. But now, after working on this manuscript — going through hundreds of pages in books, articles, reports — with all this knowledge in mind, reading these lines again, a spark of new understanding flashed. Thomas Lefroy said it: Jane was not to be easily forgotten, it was difficult to forget her — he was not able to forget her. I have now understood — but also James Edward had understood — and forgiven. The old feud between the Austen and the Lefroy families was ended...

Notes

1. It is worth mentioning that in a first version, later to be replaced by chapters 23 and 24, this sentence already existed and it is the only one to be taken over in the last version, which proves its importance.

2. The white coats were inspired by his admiration of Tom Jones who was anything but an austere Calvinist!

3. After Anna Austen married Ben Lefroy we may presume that news from the Austen family reached Thomas Lefroy more easily and that in 1816 he came to know that Jane was seriously ill.

4. Three days before her death Jane Austen composed a poem inspired by her amusement that St Swithin's Day, traditionally rainy, was by custom the day of Winchester races. It is a proof that she kept her sense of humour to the very last.

Bibliography

Austen-Leigh, J. E., *A Memoir*, (1869), Penguin, 1986
Austen, Jane *Lady Susan, The Watsons, Sanditon*, Penguin, 1974
Austen, Jane *Northanger Abbey*, Penguin, 1987
Austen, Jane *Sense and Sensibility*, Penguin, 1976
Austen, Jane *Pride and Prejudice*, Brown, Watson Ltd., London, 1968
Austen, Jane *Mansfield Park*, Penguin, 1986
Austen, Jane *Persuasion*, Penguin, 1986
Brontë, Charlotte *Jane Eyre*, Penguin, 1979
Austen, Caroline *My Aunt Jane Austen*, 1867, 1953
Austen, Caroline *Reminiscences*, 1874, The Jane Austen Society, 1979
Cecil, David *A Portrait of Jane Austen*, Penguin, 1986
Freeman, Jane *Jane Austen in Bath*, 1983
Chapman, R. W., *Jane Austen's letters to her sister Cassandra and others*, Oxford University Press, 1952
Chapman, R. W., *Jane Austen, Facts and Problems*, Oxford University Press, 1948
Jenkins, Elizabeth *Jane Austen, A Biography*, Victor Gollancz Ltd., London, 1938
Wallace, Robert K., *Jane Austen and Mozart — Classical Equilibrium in Fiction and Music*, The University of Georgia Press, Athens, 1983
Wallace, Robert K., *Jane Austen's Neglected Song Book*, Annual Report of the Jane Austen Society, 1979, pp.121–5
Honan, Park *Jane Austen: Her Life*, Weidenfeld and Nicolson, 1987
Brydges, Egerton *Imaginative Biography*, 1834
Brydges, Egerton *The Autobiography*, Vols. I and II, 1834
Collected Reports of the Jane Austen Society, 1966–89
Fielding, Henry *Tom Jones*, Penguin, 1972
Lefroy, Helen *Strangers*, Reports of the Jane Austen Society, 1982
Le Faye, Deirdre *Tom Lefroy and Jane Austen*, Reports of the Jane Austen Society, 1985
Lefroy, J. A. P., *Jane Austen's Irish Friend: Rt. Hon. Thomas Langlois Lefroy 1776–1869*, Proceedings of the Huguenot Society of London, 1979, XXXIII (3) pp.148–65
Austen-Leigh, William and Austen-Leigh, Richard Arthur *Jane Austen — Her Life and Letters — a Family Record*, Smith, Elder and Co, London, 1913
Einstein, Alfred *Mozart — l'homme et l'oeuvre*, Gallimard, Paris, 1991
Richardson, Samuel *Sir Charles Grandison*, Oxford University Press, 1965
Lefroy, Thomas *Memoir of Chief Justice Lefroy*, by his son Thomas Lefroy, Dublin, 1871